Introduction to Linden Scripting Language for Second Life

Introduction to Linden Scripting Language for Second Life

by Jeff Heaton

Heaton Research, Inc.
St. Louis

Introduction to Linden Scripting Language for Second Life

Second printing

Publisher: Heaton Research, Inc

Author: Jeff Heaton

Editor: Mark Biss

Cover Art: Carrie Spear

```
ISBN's for all Editions:
1-6043900-4-2, Softcover
1-6043900-5-0, Adobe PDF e-book
```

SOFTWARE LICENSE AGREEMENT: TERMS AND CONDITIONS

WARRANTY

Heaton Research, Inc. warrants the enclosed media to be free of physical defects for a period of ninety (90) days after purchase. The Software is not available from Heaton Research, Inc. in any other form or media than that enclosed herein or posted to www.heatonresearch.com. If you discover a defect in the media during this warranty period, you may obtain a replacement of identical format at no charge by sending the defective media, postage prepaid, with proof of purchase to:

```
Heaton Research, Inc.
Customer Support Department
1734 Clarkson Rd #107
Chesterfield, MO 63017-4976

Web: www.heatonresearch.com
E-Mail: support@heatonresearch.com
```

After the 90-day period, you can obtain replacement media of identical format by sending us the defective disk, proof of purchase, and a check or money order for $10, payable to Heaton Research, Inc..

DISCLAIMER

Heaton Research, Inc. makes no warranty or representation, either expressed or implied, with respect to the Software or its contents, quality, performance, merchantability, or fitness for a particular purpose. In no event will Heaton Research, Inc., its distributors, or dealers be liable to you or any other party for direct, indirect, special, incidental, consequential, or other damages arising out of the use of or inability to use the Software or its contents even if advised of the possibility of such damage. In the event that the Software includes an online update feature, Heaton Research, Inc. further disclaims any obligation to provide this feature for any specific duration other than the initial posting.

The exclusion of implied warranties is not permitted by some states. Therefore, the above exclusion may not apply to you. This warranty provides you with specific legal rights; there may be other rights that you may have that vary from state to state. The pricing of the book with the Software by Heaton Research, Inc. reflects the allocation of risk and limitations on liability contained in this agreement of Terms and Conditions.

SHAREWARE DISTRIBUTION

This Software may contain various programs that are distributed as shareware. Copyright laws apply to both shareware and ordinary commercial software, and the copyright Owner(s) retains all rights. If you try a shareware program and continue using it, you are expected to register it. Individual programs differ on details of trial periods, registration, and payment. Please observe the requirements stated in appropriate files.

This book is dedicated to LolaLee Dibou.

Acknowledgments

There are several people who I would like to acknowledge. First, I would like to thank the many people who have given me suggestions and comments on my Second Life scripts.

I would like to thank WordsRU.com for providing editing resources. I would like to thank Mark Biss for editing the book.

I would like to thank my sister Carrie Spear for layout and formatting suggestions.

Contents at a Glance

Introduction XXXI
Chapter 1: Introduction to Second Life Building 35
Chapter 2: Introduction to LSL 51
Chapter 3: Script Control 63
Chapter 4: State Machines 75
Chapter 5: String Handling 83
Chapter 6: Communication...99
Chapter 7: Events...113
Chapter 8: Lists..131
Chapter 9: Non-Physical Movement...141
Chapter 10: Physical Movement and Vehicles.................................163
Chapter 11: Changing Object Attributes 189
Chapter 12: Using Particles 201
Appendix A: Downloading Examples 221

Contents

Introduction XXXI
Chapter 1: Introduction to Second Life Building 35
   Creating Prims...35
   Modifying Prims Visually...36
   Modifying Prims with the Properties Window.............................39
   Linking Prims 46
   Summary 47
Chapter 2: Introduction to LSL 51
   Second Life Programming 51
   Creating a Script..52
   Variables..55
   Functions 58
   Events 60
   Summary 61
Chapter 3: Script Control 63
   Using If and Else Statements 63
   Using Switch and Case 67
   Using Loops 68
   Summary 71
Chapter 4: State Machines 75
   What is a State Machine? 75
   Understanding Second Life State Machines 76
   Life With and Without State Machines..77
   Summary 80
Chapter 5: String Handling 83
   String Functions 83
   String Comparison...84
   Using Notecards 91
   Summary 96
Chapter 6: Communication 99
   Speaking and Listening 99

Understanding Dialogs...103
Instant Messages 104
Setting Prim Text 107
Linked Messages..108
Summary 111
Chapter 7: Events...113
Timer Events 113
Collision Events 114
Sensor Events 116
Money Events 119
Handling Permissions 122
Implementing Basic Security...125
Summary 128
Chapter 8: Lists..131
Adding and Removing Items to Lists..131
Retrieving Data from Lists 132
Lists and CSV...134
List Statistics...136
Sorting, Searching and Striding Lists.......................................138
Summary 139
Chapter 9: Non-Physical Movement...141
Second Life Coordinates 141
Displaying an Object's Location and Rotation 144
Changing and Object's Location and Rotation.........................146
A Touring Balloon 147
Summary 161
Chapter 10: Physical Movement and Vehicles...........................163
Applying Force to an Avatar..163
Applying Force to the Current Object 166
Second Life Vehicles 168
Summary 186
Chapter 11: Changing Object Attributes 189
Using llSetPrimitiveParams 189
Using llGetPrimitiveParams 197
Using llSetLinkPrimitiveParams 198
Setting Attribute Properties 198
Summary 199
Chapter 12: Using Particles 201

Basic Particle Emitter..201
A Fog Machine 208
Snowflake Emitter...213
Summary 218
Appendix A: Downloading Examples 221

Table of Figures

Figure 1.1: The Build Window 36
Figure 1.2: Editing a Prim's Position 37
Figure 1.3: Editing a Prim's Size 38
Figure 1.4: Editing a Prim's Rotation 39
Figure 1.5: The General Properties of a Prim 40
Figure 1.6: The Object Properties of a Prim 41
Figure 1.7: The Features Properties of a Prim 42
Figure 1.8: The Textures Properties of a Prim 43
Figure 1.9: The Content Properties of a Prim 44
Figure 1.10: A New Script 45
Figure 1.11: Linking a Snowman..46
Figure 1.12: The Root Prim of the Snowman 47
Figure 2.1: A New Script 53
Figure 2.2: The Script Editor 54
Figure 4.1: A State Machine...76
Figure 5.1: Creating a Notecard 91
Figure 6.1: Conversation on Channel 0 100
Figure 6.2: Second Life Dialogs...103
Figure 6.3: Prim Text...107
Figure 6.4: A Simple Linked Object 109
Figure 7.1: A Payment Dialog 121
Figure 7.2: Money Dialog 122
Figure 7.3: Setting the Group of an Object..127
Figure 9.1: Gyeonu and Surrounding Regions 142
Figure 9.2: Encogia Island 143
Figure 9.3: The Coordinate System 144
Figure 9.4: A Touring Balloon...148
Figure 10.1: A Trampoline 164
Figure 10.2: Marking an Object as Physical 166
Figure 10.3: A Car in Second Life 168
Figure 10.4: Setting the Material Type 169

Figure 10.5: A Car with Two Passengers.......................................182
Figure 12.1: Basic Particle Emitter...202
Figure 12.2: A Fog Machine 209
Figure 12.3: Snowflake Texture..213
Figure 12.4: A Snowflake Emitter...214

Table of Listings

Listing 2.1: Display Variable 56
Listing 2.2: Script Level Variables 57
Listing 2.3: Simple Function 58
Listing 2.4: Functions with Parameters 59
Listing 2.5: Function that Returns Values 59
Listing 3.1: A Hello Script 63
Listing 3.2: A While Loop 69
Listing 3.3: A While Loop Counts Backwards 69
Listing 3.4: A Do/While Loop 70
Listing 3.5: A Do/While Loop That Executes Once 70
Listing 3.6: A For Loop 71
Listing 4.1: Programming without State Machines 77
Listing 4.2: Programming with State Machines 78
Listing 4.3: State events 78
Listing 5.1: String Comparison 84
Listing 5.2: A Simple Notecard 92
Listing 5.3: Reading Notecards 92
Listing 6.1: Say Hello 101
Listing 6.2: Instant Message 102
Listing 6.3: A Second Life Dialog..103
Listing 6.4: A Simple Pager...105
Listing 6.5: The Green Button 109
Listing 6.6: The Red Button 110
Listing 6.7: The Root Prim that Receives the Messages 110
Listing 7.1: Timer Events 113
Listing 7.2: Working with Collisions...115
Listing 7.3: A Water Splash...116
Listing 7.4: Notecard Giver 117
Listing 7.5: Tip Jar 119
Listing 7.6: Guessing Game 122
Listing 7.7: Owner Security 125
Listing 7.8: Group Security 127
Listing 8.1: Dumping List Data 133
Listing 8.2: Display a List 134
Listing 8.3: Convert a List to CSV 135
Listing 8.4: Convert CSV to a List...135

Listing 8.5: Getting List Statistics 137
Listing 9.1: Display Current Position...145
Listing 9.2: Display the Current Rotation 145
Listing 9.3: Changing Object Location 146
Listing 9.4: Changing Object Rotation 146
Listing 9.5: Rotation with llTargetOmega.......................................147
Listing 9.6: Configuring the Balloon...148
Listing 9.7: A Touring Balloon...149
Listing 9.8: Balloon Seat Script..159
Listing 10.1: Trampoline Script...164
Listing 10.2: Main Car Script for the Root Prim (Car.lsl) 171
Listing 10.3: Car Passenger Seat (CarSeat.lsl) 183
Listing 10.4: Can't Sit Here (DontSitHere.lsl) 183
Listing 10.5: Car Wheel (WheelScript.lsl)......................................184
Listing 10.6: Rotate the Hubcaps (WheelScript.lsl) 185
Listing 11.1: Random Color Cube...198
Listing 12.1: Basic Particle Emitter (BasicParticle.lsl) 202
Listing 12.2: A Fog Machine 209
Listing 12.3: snowflake Emitter 214

XXVII

Table of Tables

Table 2.1: Variable Types 55
Table 5.1: Linden String Functions...84
Table 6.1: Communication Distances...102
Table 6.2: Message Target Types...110
Table 8.1: Accessing Data in a List 133
Table 8.2: Accessing Data in a List 136
Table 8.3: Statistic Types 136
Table 10.1: Vehicle Types 178
Table 10.2: Floating Point Vehicle Parameters................................179
Table 10.3: Vector Vehicle Parameters 180
Table 11.1: Constants for llSetPrimitiveParams 191
Table 11.2: PRIM_TYPE Constants 193
Table 11.3: Holeshape Constants 195
Table 11.4: Bumpmapping Constants 196
Table 11.5: Shininess Constants 196
Table 11.6: Material Constants 197
Table 12.1: PSYS_PART_FLAGS Flags 205
Table 12.2: PSYS_SRC_PATTERN Values......................................206
Table 12.3: Remaining Particle Emitter Name-Value Pairs 207
Table 12.4: Fog Machine Attributes...212
Table 12.5: Snowflake Emitter Attributes 217

INTRODUCTION

The Linden Scripting Language allows residents of the Second Life World to program the three dimensional objects around them. Without this programming objects built in Second Life are motionless and non-interactive. Adding a script enables an object to interact with the world around it. Second Life scripts allow objects such as cars, planes, amusement park rides, weapons and other entertainment devices to be created.

This book teaches the beginning Second Life programmer to make use of the basics of the Linden Scripting Language. Language fundamentals, such as variables, loops, lists, events, functions and state machines are covered. The book then moves to more advanced topics such as user interaction and non-physical movement. Later chapters show how to use the Second Life physics engine to create vehicles.

To script in Second Life, one must know the basics of building. Chapter 1 begins with a basic introduction to building. You are shown how to create prims and link them to form objects. Rotation, position, and other more advanced attributes of prims are covered.

Chapter 2 begins with an introduction to the Linden Scripting Language. You are shown how to create scripts and perform basic operations. This chapter introduces variables and shows the structure of a script.

Chapter 3 focuses on script control. You will see how to cause your scripts to make decisions based on variables. You will also see how to use the three different loop types that Second Life makes available.

Second Life makes extensive use of state machines. Chapter 4 is exclusively dedicated to state machines. You will see how to make use of state machines in a script. You will see how to initialize a state and switch between states.

Strings hold textual information. Chapter 5 shows how to manipulate strings. You will see how to compare strings, beyond the simple case sensitive comparisons provided by the Linden Scripting Language. You will also see how to parse strings.

Object can communicate in nearly all of the ways that avatars communicate. Chapter 6 shows how to send instant messages, as well as communicate publicly with all avatars around. Additionally, Second Life menus are covered.

Events are special functions that are called when something happens. Though events were mentioned in pervious chapters, Chapter 7 looks at evens in greater detail. You will also see how to use scanner and money events.

The Linden Scripting Language does not support arrays. Chapter 8 covers lists, which is what the Linden Scripting uses to hold collection of items.

Chapters 9 and 10 cover physical and non-physical movement. Non-physical movement works by changing the x, y and z-coordinates of an object. Physical movement applies a force to the object and uses the laws of physics to move that object.

Chapter 11 shows how to modify prims. Prims can be modified by the script. Any attribute that can be set visually, while building, can also be set by a script. This allows objects to change attributes, such as their image textures, dynamically.

Chapter 12 covers particles. Particles are 2D objects that are often used to cause objects to shine, burn or produce smoke. A variety of effects can be achieved using particles.

The examples are listed in this book. However, it is not necessary to type them out. All recipes can be obtained, from Second Life, in fully working form. To obtain any of the recipes, visit the Heaton Research HQ on Encogia Island. The Heaton Research HQ can be found at the following location.

`http://slurl.com/secondlife/Encogia/200/196/23`

`http://www.heatonresearch.com/download/`

CHAPTER 1: INTRODUCTION TO SECOND LIFE BUILDING

- Creating Primitive Objects
- Modifying Primitive Objects
- Primitive Object Properties
- Linking Primitive Objects

This book explains how to program in the Linden Scripting Language. However, scripts are always attached to a 3D object that was built by someone. This chapter will present a basic overview of building in Second Life. Before learning to create scripts in Second Life, it is very important to understand the basics of building objects.

Objects in Second Life are composed of primitive objects. Each primitive object in Second Life represents a basic geometric shape. These primitive objects, or prims, are linked to form bigger objects. The next section will explain how to create prims.

Creating Prims

To create a prim you must be in building mode. To enter build mode, click the build button near the bottom of the Second Life screen. If the build button is disabled, you do not have sufficient rights to build on the land that you are currently standing on. The owner of the land can set the land permissions however they please.

If you do not own any land in Second Life, you will need to build at a sandbox. A sandbox is a public area where everyone is allowed to build. To find a sandbox, use the search button to search for "sandbox".

Once the build button is successfully clicked, the build window will appear. The build window can be seen in Figure 1.1.

Figure 1.1: The Build Window

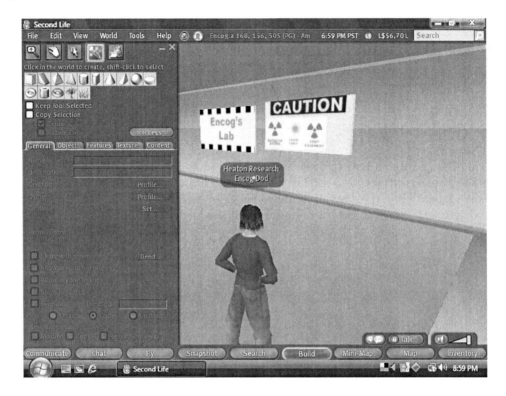

As can be seen from the build window, a number of different geometric prims can be created. Select the geometric figure that you would like to begin your object with. Creating an object in Second Life is a process of creating geometric primitives and then linking them. After the geometric primitive has been selected, the mouse cursor will look like a "magic wand". Move the "magic wand" to where the prim should be created and click the mouse. The prim will be created.

Modifying Prims Visually

After the prim has been created, it can be modified. There are two primary ways to modify a prim in Second Life. Firstly, the prim can be modified visually, through the use of the mouse. Secondly, the prim can be modified directly by editing its values in the prim's properties window. This section describes how to modify the prims visually.

Three attributes can be edited visually using the mouse. These attributes are:

• position
• size
• rotation

In the following sections you will learn how to visually modify each of the above attributes.

Visually Editing a Prim's Position

When a prim is selected red, green and blue arrows will appear around the prim. These arrows can be used to change the position of the prim. Drag the arrow that is pointing in the direction you want the prim to be moved. The arrow can then be used to move the prim. Figure 1.2 shows a prim having its position changed visually.

Figure 1.2: Editing a Prim's Position

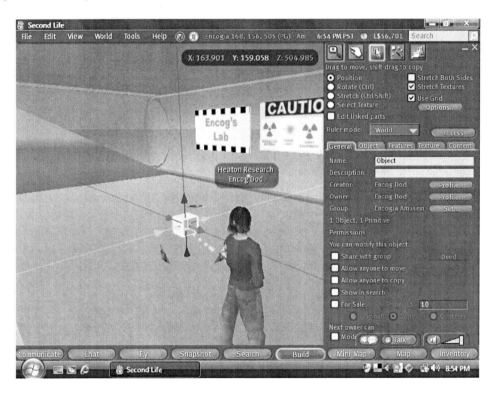

The prim can now be dragged in any of the three dimensions by dragging the arrows around the object.

Visually Editing a Prim's Size

When a prim is selected, holding down the ctrl-shift will replace the red, green and blue position arrows with red, green and blue resize boxes. A prim with resize boxes can be seen in Figure 1.3.

Figure 1.3: Editing a Prim's Size

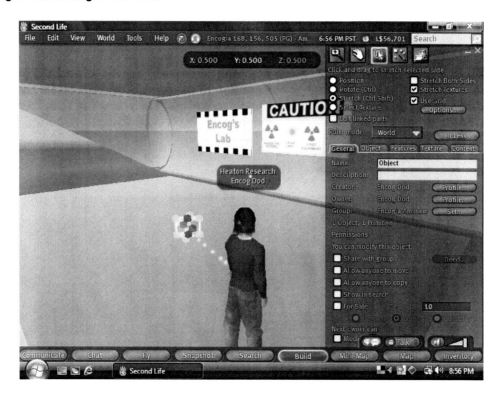

By dragging the resize boxes, the prim can be resized.

Visually Editing a Prim's Rotation

It is also possible to visually rotate a prim. When a prim is selected, holding down the ctrl key will replace the red, green and blue position arrows with red, green and blue rotation arrows.

Figure 1.4: Editing a Prim's Rotation

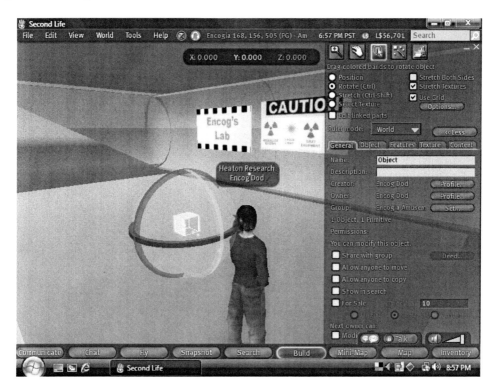

By dragging the rotation arrows, the prim can be rotated.

Modifying Prims with the Properties Window

It is also possible to modify many of the properties of a prim by editing the prim's properties window. Right-clicking a prim and then selecting "Edit" will bring up the prim's properties window. Figure 1.5 shows the properties window for a prim.

Figure 1.5: The General Properties of a Prim

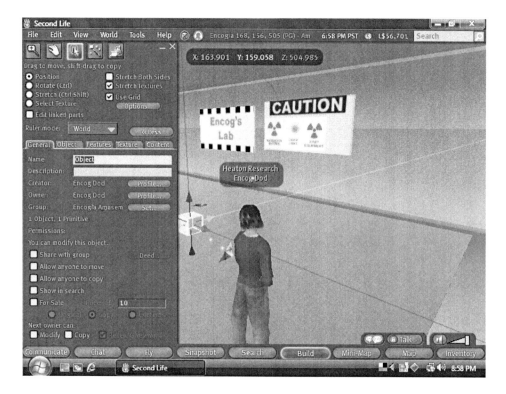

When editing a prim the properties window will appear. There are several tabs that can be selected to edit different aspects of the prim. The tabs that appear with any prim are shown here.

- General
- Object
- Features
- Texture
- Content

Each of these tabs allows a different set of properties to be edited. The next few sections describe how to edit the properties on each of these tabs.

General Prim Properties

The general properties are shown in Figure 1.5. The general properties allow basic properties, such as the prim's name and description to be edited. The primitive's owner and creator are also shown. The creator of a prim can never be edited. However, it is possible to change the owner of a prim by selling that prim.

There are checkboxes that allow the permissions of the prim to be set. These allow the next owner to copy, modify or sell/give away the prim. You can also define what other uses are allowed to do to this prim.

Object Prim Properties

The object properties tab allows the size, position, rotation and other important properties of a prim to be edited. Figure 1.6 shows the object properties of a prim.

Figure 1.6: The Object Properties of a Prim

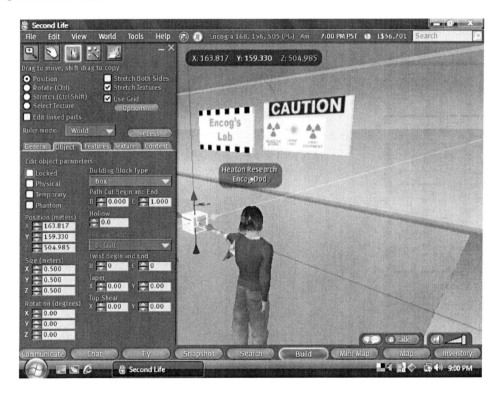

The object and texture properties are the two tabs most commonly used for Second Life building. The object tab allows the x, y and z values for the position, size and rotation to be specified. The visual method of adjusting size, rotation and position is often used, but then the numbers are adjusted so that they are even. For example, if I rotate a prim to 93 degrees visually, I will edit the 93 degrees to be 90 degrees. This allows all of my angles to be "true" and produces a more "mathematically perfect" final object.

Other properties, such as path cut, hollow, twist, taper and top shear can bend, twist and hollow the object. The best way to get a feel for these properties is to place a simple prim and then adjust the properties and observe the effect.

The material type of a prim can also be defined. Wood is the default material type. Most objects created in Second Life never change the material type. As a result, most of the Second Life world is made of wood. The material property is really only useful for defining the friction between the prim and other prims. For example, glass has very little friction, whereas rubber has a great deal of friction. Friction will become very important later in this book when "physical" objects, such as vehicles, are created.

Features Prim Properties

The features prim properties tab allows lighting and flexible path options to be set. Figure 1.7 shows the features properties tab.

Figure 1.7: The Features Properties of a Prim

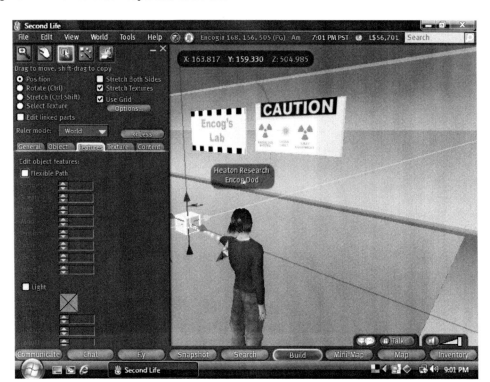

There are two check boxes, as seen on Figure 1.7. The first check box, the flexible path, allows a prim to be flexible. A flexible prim flexes in response to wind, movement and gravity. Flexible prims are used to create flags, flexible hair, and flexible clothing in Second Life.

The second Check Box, light, allows the prim to emit light. Various options can be defined for light, such as color, intensity, radius and falloff. The light produced by a prim is most clearly visable at night.

Texture Prim Properties

The textures properties tab of the prim properties window allows the texture for a prim to be defined. The texture of a prim defines what material the prim appears to be made of. The textures property tab can be seen in Figure 1.8.

Figure 1.8: The Textures Properties of a Prim

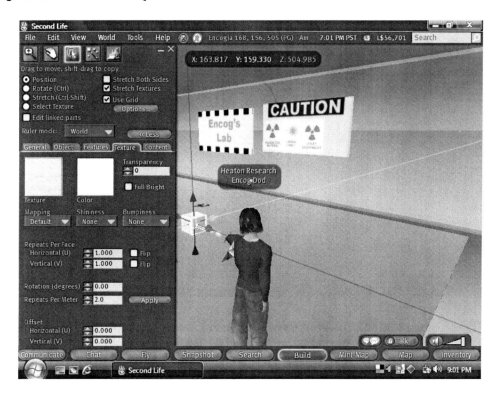

As can be seen from the above properties tab, the texture can be selected as well as the color. To create a solid color prim, choose the texture "blank" and then select the color. The shininess of the texture can also be chosen. This allows some interesting effects to be created. Shininess can also be defined for prims. The textures can also be scaled and offset.

Content Prim Properties

The content properties tab for a prim allows objects to be placed inside the prim. This is where scripts are added. Figure 1.9 shows the content properties of a prim.

Figure 1.9: The Content Properties of a Prim

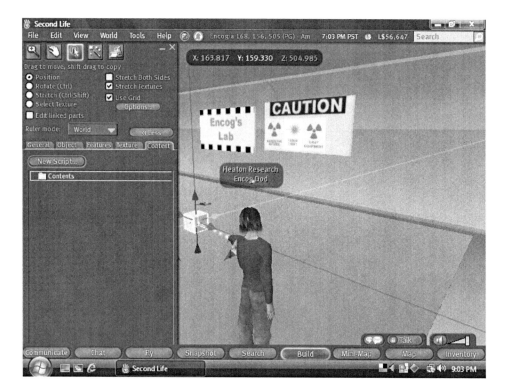

Objects placed into the content tab of the prim have no effect on the visual appearance of the prim. Objects placed here are used by the scripts that execute within the prim. Each prim can have several scripts that execute. Objects in Second Life are usually made of a number of linked prims. Each of these linked prims can have its own set of content.

Content includes scripts and everything needed by scripts. Audio files, scripts, textures and other objects can all be included in an object. Later chapters will show how to use some of these objects in conjunction with a script. To create a script in an object, right-click the object and choose "Edit". Then choose the "Content" tab of the prim properties window. Press the "New Script" button. A new script is created, as shown in Figure 1.10.

Figure 1.10: A New Script

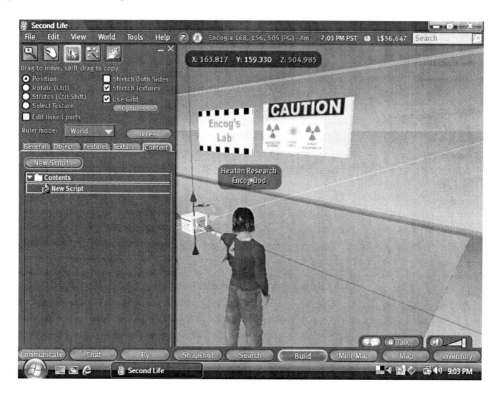

Second Life provides default code for the script. This **default** script can be seen by double-clicking the "New Script" shown in Figure 1.10. The **default** script can be seen here.

```
default
{
    state_entry()
    {
        llSay(0, "Hello, Avatar!");
    }

    touch_start(integer total_number)
    {
        llSay(0, "Touched.");
    }
}
```

The **default** script does very little, it is simply a placeholder until a more complex script is created.

Linking Prims

Prims can be linked. When several prims are linked, they move together. This is how larger, more complex objects are created in Second Life. To link more than one object in Second Life, select multiple objects and choose the "Link" option from the "Tools" menu. To select more than one object begin by selecting the first object, and then hold down the "Shift" key to select additional objects. The additional objects will be highlighted in yellow. Figure 1.11 shows three "snow balls" of a snowman about to be linked.

Figure 1.11: Linking a Snowman

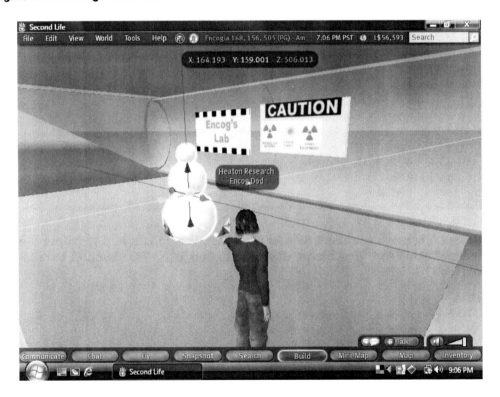

Objects can also be unlinked. Select one, or more prims of the linked object. If you would like to select individual prims of a linked object, the "Edit linked parts" check box on the build window must be checked. Once the prims to be unlinked have been selected, choose the "Unlink" item from the "Tools" menu.

Not all prims in a linked object are equal. One special prim is called the "root prim". The root prim is the prim that all movement to the object occurs on. You can think of the root prim as what is actually moving, everything else is simply attached to the root prim. When vehicles and physical objects are created, the root prim becomes very important. All rotation to the compound object is performed on the root prim, the other parts simply follow.

The root prim is always the last prim that was added to an object. You can easily view the root prim by selecting an object. All non-root prims will show up as cyan. The root prim will show up as yellow. Figure 1.12 shows the snowman. The base of the snowman is the root prim. As you can see, from Figure 1.12, the base of the snowman is outlined in yellow.

Figure 1.12: The Root Prim of the Snowman

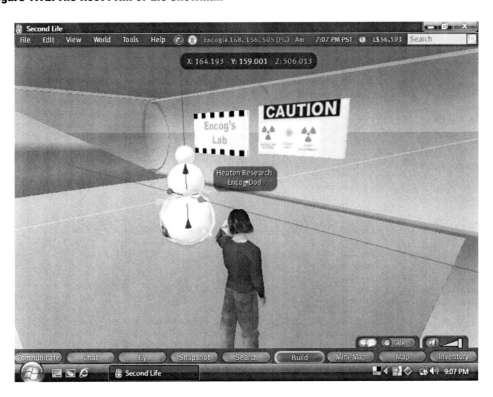

Summary

This book is primarily about scripting which requires some basic building knowledge. This chapter introduced the basics of building in Second Life.

Objects in Second Life are created by linking prims. Prims are basic geometric shapes that form the building blocks of more complex Second Life objects. When prims are linked together, the last prim selected becomes the root prim for the object. All motion occurs on the root prim, the other prims act as if they are attached to the root prim.

The Linden Scripting Language allows computer programs to be embedded in the 3D objects that make up the Second Life world. These programs define how the Second Life objects interact with the world around them. The next chapter will introduce the Linden Scripting Language.

Chapter 2: Introduction to LSL

- Using Scripts
- Understanding Variables
- Processing Events

Second Life (SL) is an extremely popular, massively-multiplayer online game (MMOG). Many consider Second Life to be much more than a game. Second Life is somewhat like the movie "The Matrix," in which people live and work in a simulated world. Second Life is very similar; your computer player, called an avatar, lives in Second Life's 3D world.

However, unlike "The Matrix," current computer technology is not sufficiently advanced to comprehensively simulate a physical world. This means Second Life has two shortcomings.

First, you see the world of Second Life through a computer screen, which - even though it uses state-of-the-art 3D graphics - gives the simulation a cartoonish look. Despite this, many areas in Second Life are visually stunning.

Second, the simulation of Second Life is not a complete physical simulation. Important elements, including gravity, are present. However, you could not completely simulate something as complex as an automobile in Second Life. It's still too difficult to simulate all the aspects of the internal combustion engine and electrical components of a car. Modern computers are not powerful enough to do this. Still, there are cars and many other sorts of vehicles in Second Life. The gap between real physics and Second Life physics is bridged using scripts created in Second Life.

Second Life Programming

Second Life provides a scripting programming language called the Linden Scripting Language (LSL) to fill in the gaps left by Second Life's simple physics engine. Rather than simulate every aspect of a car, a programmer creates a script that tells the car how it should move. This script can play sounds, turn the car and even detect collisions. For example, to add realism, a car script could prevent the car from turning when not in motion.

This book provides an introduction to LSL. For you to obtain the greatest benefit, I recommend that you have a basic knowledge of "building", but that's not required to understand the book's code. Building is the process by which you place 3D primitives into the Second Life world. Builders have created everything that you see in Second Life.

The Linden Scripting Language looks much like C at first glance. However, it is much easier to program than C. There are no pointers and you can do direct string comparisons without using functions such as **strcmp**. LSL is not object-oriented; you cannot create your own objects, and the language provides only a few 3D-related objects for you. LSL is state based. Every LSL script has a specific state and carries out its functions by moving through a series of states. This is quite a different concept from most programming languages. While you can build state machines in most languages, in LSL the concept of a state machine is inherently part of the language.

LSL scripts reside inside 3D primitives in Second Life. Objects are collections of primitives. For example, a car in Second Life would be a single object. However, the car object would be made up of many primitives, each of which may contain its own script. Additionally, these primitives can communicate with each other or even with human players. With more advanced programming, primitives can even communicate with web pages external to Second Life.

LSL is also event driven. Most objects in Second Life work by progressing through states driven by events. Second Life provides many different event types. Most are user-based, such as when a user touches or sits on an object; however, it also supports timer events that require no user interaction.

Creating a Script

Second Life scripts are contained in prims. Each prim can contain one or more scripts. To create a simple script, rez a cube onto the ground. Edit the cube and select the "Content" tab. If you do not see the "Content" tab, select the "More>>>" button. The Content tab shows all of the items contained inside of the box. Prims can contain many different types of objects. Prims can also contain other prims.

Prims usually contain scripts and other objects useful to those scripts. For example, an automobile may contain a script to run the car. The automobile might also contain sounds to play when the car is started or shut off. To create a new script in the box that was just rezzed, select the "New Script..." button. This will add a script named "New Script" to the content pane. This script can be seen in Figure 2.1.

Figure 2.1: A New Script

To edit the script, double click the new script. This will open the script editor. The script editor can be seen in Figure 2.2.

Figure 2.2: The Script Editor

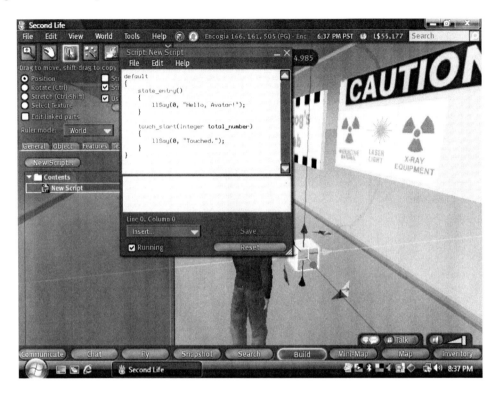

Whenever a new script is created a "generic script" is placed inside of the script. This "generic script" can be seen in Figure 2.2. This is the starting point for all scripts created in Second Life. One of the first things to notice about the script, shown in Figure 2.2, is the use of curly braces. Second Life scripts are broken into blocks of code. These blocks begin with an opening curly brace ({) and end with a closing curly brace (}).

A block of code can contain other blocks of code. For example, Figure 2.2 shows a block of code named **default**. The word "default" appears just before the opening curly brace. Inside of the default block of code there are two other blocks of code. The first is named **state_entry**. The second is named **touch_start**. The **default** block of code contains the other two blocks of code.

Blocks of code group the code contained within them together. The **default** block of code defines one state of the script. Scripts in Second Life are implemented as state machines. Scripts begin in the **default** state and each script must provide a **default** state. .Scripts are not required to contain any state other than the **default** state. For the script shown in Figure 2.2 there is only the **default** state. State machines will be covered in Chapter 4.

Variables

Variables allow a script to hold information. Unlike many scripting languages, Second Life variables are strongly typed. For example, to declare an **integer**, named **i**, use the following code.

```
integer i;
```

Once declared, the variable can be assigned using the equals operator. For example, to assign the variable **i** to the value of zero, the following code would be used.

```
i = 0;
```

Values can also be added to i as follows:

```
i = i + 1;
```

The above expression can also be expressed with the following shorthand:

```
i+=i;
```

Additionally, if the value of **i** is to be incremented by only one, the following shorthand can be used:

```
i++;
```

Second Life supports a number of variable types. These types are summarized in Table 2.1.

Table 2.1: Variable Types

Type	Description
integer	A whole number ranging from -2,147,483,648 to 2,147,483,647.
float	A decimal number ranging from 1.175494351E-38 to 3.402823466E+38.
vector	Three floats in the form < x , y , z >. Usually a position, color, or Euler rotation.
rotation	A quaternion rotation, made up of 4 floats, < x , y , z , s >
key	A UUID (specialized string) used to identify something in SL, notably an agent, object, sound, texture, other inventory item, or dataserver request
string	A sequence of characters, limited only by the amount of free memory available to the script.
list	A heterogeneous list of the other data types.

The two numeric types are **integer** and **float**. The type of **integer** should be used when no decimal places are required. If decimal places are required, then the numeric type, **float**, should be used. The other variable types, described in Table 2.1, will be described in later chapters.

A variable's scope defines from where the variable may be accessed. The Linden Scripting Language supports two levels of variable scope. Variable scope will be explained in the next section.

Variable Scope Types

Declaring a variable in a script does not necessarily make that variable accessible from anywhere in the script. The accessibility of a variable is referred to as variable scope. Where the variable is defined at determines the variable's scope. There are two types of variable scope in Second Life.

- Local Variables, and
- Script-Level Variables

The next two sections will describe each of these scope types.

Local Variables

Local variables are variables defined inside of a function. These variables can only be accessed from within the function they were declared in. Also, they can only be accessed by parts of the function further down than where they were declared. For example, consider the following script that displays the value of the **i** variable.

Listing 2.1: Display Variable

```
default
{
    touch_start(integer total_number)
    {
        integer i;
        i=0;
        llSay(0, "The value of i is: " + (string)i);
    }
}
```

The above code is inside if the function **touch_start**. This is a special type of function, called an event. Events and functions will be explained later in this chapter. Events and functions are blocks of code that are called at certain times. The **touch_start** event is called whenever an avatar touches the object containing the script.

First the **integer i** is declared. Next the variable is assigned a value of zero. This object then "says" what the value of the variable is. Notice the **llSay** function call. This is very important, as it is how many of the early programs in this book will communicate. Using the **llSay** function, an object can communicate in a similar manner to an avatar. The first parameter to **llSay** specifies the channel. Channel zero means that every avatar around will hear the communication. Sometimes objects will want to communicate with each other over private channels. To display the variable, a typecast of **(string)** is used to covert it to a string.

It is very important to use the variable only after it has been declared. The following script is invalid because the variable is displayed before it has been declared.

```
default
{
    touch_start(integer total_number)
    {
        llSay(0, "The value of i is: " + (string)i);

        integer i;
        i=0;
    }
}
```

Additionally, other functions cannot access the local variable declared inside of other functions.

Script-Level Variables

Local variables are limited in their scope. They can only be accessed within a single function. Additionally, the value of a local variable is reset each time the function is called. This can be very limiting. Often a script will want to hold onto values indefinitely. Script-level variables hold their values indefinitely and they can be accessed by any function in the script. The following shows a script-level variable, named **count**, being used.

Listing 2.2: Script Level Variables

```
integer count;

default
{
    state_entry()
    {
        count = 0;
    }

    touch_start(integer total_number)
    {
```

```
        count ++;
        llSay(0, "Count: " + (string)count);
    }
}
```

The above code implements a simple counter. The counter is reset to zero when the script first starts. When the **default** state is entered, the **state_entry** event function is called. In this function the **count** variable is reset to zero. Each time the object is touched the **touch_start** event function will be called. This will increment the **count** variable and the value of the **count** variable is then displayed.

Notice where the **count** variable is declared. Placing the **count** variable's declaration outside of any state causes the variable to be script-level.

Functions

A function is a named block of code that can be called from elsewhere in the script. First we will examine a simple function that accepts no parameters and does not return anything. The following code demonstrates this.

Listing 2.3: Simple Function

```
integer count;

display()
{
    llSay(0, "Count: " + (string)count);
}

default
{
    state_entry()
    {
        count = 0;
    }

    touch_start(integer total_number)
    {
        count ++;
        display();
    }
}
```

The above code defines a function named **display**. Notice where the function is declared. It is declared outside of any state. Functions cannot be defined inside of a state. Only events can be defined inside of a state. Events will be covered in the next section.

The above function simply displays the count. The new function is called by the following line of code.

```
display();
```

Functions can also accept parameters. The following script demonstrates a function that accepts one parameter.

Listing 2.4: Functions with Parameters

```
integer count;

display(integer i)
{
    llSay(0, "Count: " + (string)i);
}

default
{
    state_entry()
    {
        count = 0;
    }

    touch_start(integer total_number)
    {
        count ++;
        display(count);
    }
}
```

The **display** function accepts a single parameter named **i**. This parameter is the value that is to be displayed. To call a function with a parameter the following code is used.

```
display(count);
```

As can be seen, the **count** variable is passed into the **display** function. It is not possible for a function to modify the variable that was passed to it.

Functions can also return values. The following script demonstrates how to use a function that accepts two parameters and returns a value.

Listing 2.5: Function that Returns Values

```
integer count;

integer multiply(integer x,integer y)
{
    integer result = x * y;
```

```
        return result;
}

default
{
    state_entry()
    {
        count = 0;
    }

    touch_start(integer total_number)
    {
        integer x = multiply(5,10);
        llSay(0, "Result: " + (string)x);
    }
}
```

The above script declares the **multiply** function to return an **integer**. Did you notice the keyword **integer** before the "multiply" function name? This specifies the type that the function should return. Once a type is specified, the function must contain a **return** statement. The return statement specifies what value should be returned to the caller of the function. The following line of code calls the multiply function.

```
integer x = multiply(5,10);
```

The parameters 5 and 10 are passed into the function. The multiply function then multiplies these two numbers and returns the result. The asterisk (*) operator is used to multiply. The slash (/) operator is used to divide.

Events

Events are a special type of function. Events are the only functions that are allowed inside of a state. Event functions are not usually called by other functions. Event functions are called by Second Life itself. Second Life calls an event function when something happens that might be of interest to the script. Usually events are called because of some interaction on the scripted object either by the Second Life world or another use.

Events have very specific names. This name tells Second Life what event type this function is designed to handle. So far this chapter has used two specific events: **touch_start** and **state_entry**.

The **touch_start** event is called by Second Life whenever an avatar touches an object. If you need to know when the avatar has simply clicked an object, **touch_start** can be used. There is also a **touch_end**. The **touch_end** event is used when you need to track how long the avatar has touched an object.

The **state_entry** event function is called whenever a new state is entered. When multiple states are created, each state will usually have a **state_entry** event function to setup for that state.

There are many more event types in Second Life than were covered here. Events will be covered in much greater detail in Chapter 7.

Summary

The Linden Scripting Language (LSL) is used to create objects in Second Life that interact with the world around them. LSL is often used to overcome shortcomings in the Second Life physics engine. This book will introduce LSL.

Scripts can be created inside of any prim in Second Life. Once a Script is created in a prim, that script can be edited to produce the desired functionality. Script programming is done completely inside of the Second Life world. This chapter introduced fundamental concepts such as variables and functions.

The next chapter will expand on this one by showing how to create scripts that can make decisions. Fundamental LSL statements that allow these decisions to be made will be introduced.

CHAPTER 3: SCRIPT CONTROL

- If/Else Statements
- While Loops
- Do/While Loops
- For Loops

There are many control statements that can be used to allow scripts to make decisions. The Linden Scripting Language provides several statements that allow the execution of a script to be controlled. Parts of the script can be selectively executed based on input criteria. Loops can also be used to execute certain parts of the script a number of times. This chapter will explain how to control scripts in this way.

In this chapter **if/else** statements will be introduced. These allow a script to make decisions. **For**, **while** and **do/while** loops will be introduced to allow your scripts to repeatedly execute a block of code.

Using If and Else Statements

If/else statements allow the script to make decisions. These decisions are usually based on variables. An **if** statement will execute a block of code if the statement evaluates to **true**. An **else** statement can be used in conjunction with the **if** statement. If the **if** statement evaluates to **false**, the **if** statement's **else** statement will be executed. Not all **if** statements will have an else statement. The **else** statement is optional.

The next section will show how to use **if** statements.

Understanding If-Statements

Consider a simple script that will say hello to any avatar that says hello to the object containing the script. Such a script is shown in Listing 3.1.

Listing 3.1: A Hello Script

```
default
{
    state_entry()
    {
        llListen(0, "", NULL_KEY, "");
    }

    listen(integer channel, string name, key id, string message)
    {
        if( llToUpper(message) == "HELLO" )
        {
            llSay(0,"Hello " + name );
        }
    }
}
```

The **state_entry** event is called first. This event uses the **llListen** function call to request that the **listen** event be called whenever something is said near the object that contains the script. The first parameter to **llListen** specifies that the script should listen on channel zero. The second parameter specifies the avatar to listen for. Because an empty string is specified, the script will listen to all avatars. The third parameter allows an avatar to be specified by **key**. The fourth parameter specifies the message desired. If a value is specified for the fourth parameter, only messages that exactly match that value will be received.

Every time that something is said near the script, the **listen** event will be called. The **listen** event uses an **if** statement to look for the world "hello". Notice how the **if** statement uses the **llToUpper** function. This allows the script to be able to respond for "Hello", "hello", "HELLO" or any other combination of capital and lower case letters. Also notice the double equal (==). This specifies that this is a comparison. A single equal (=) is only used to assign a value to a variable.

An **if** statement can also be used with numbers. For example, to check to see whether the variable **a** is equal to 10, the following statement would be used.

```
if( a == 10 )
{
  llSay(0,"a is 10");
}
```

It is also possible to use comparison operators other than equal. To see whether the variable **a** is not equal to ten, the following code is used.

```
if( a != 10 )
{
   llSay(0,"a is not 10");
}
```

Greater than and less than can also be used. The following code checks to see whether the variable **a** is greater than ten.

```
if( a > 10 )
{
   llSay(0,"a is greater than 10");
}
```

Greater than or equal can be used as well. The following code checks to see whether the variable a is greater than or equal to ten.

```
if( a >= 10 )
{
   llSay(0,"a is greater than or equal to 10");
}
```

It is also possible to use boolean logic in an **if** statement. This will be explained in the next section.

Using Boolean Logic

Boolean logic can also be used with an **if** statement. The and (**&&**) and or(**||**) operators allow two comparisons to be used in an **if** statement. For example to check whether the variable a is equal to 5 or 6, the following code could be used.

```
if( a==5 || a==6 )
{
   llSay(0,"a is 5 or 6");
}
```

The or statement requires only one half of the expression to be true. If the variable **a** is equal to 5 or the variable **a** is equal to 6, then the **if** statement will execute.

The and operator is much more selective. The following **if** statement checks to see whether the variable **a** is greater than 5, yet less than 10.

```
if( a>5 && a<10 )
{
  llSay(0,"a is greater than 5 and less than 10");
}
```

For this **if** statement to execute, the variable must be greater than five, as well as less than ten. If just one of these requirements is not met, the **if** statement will not execute.

Understanding Else-Statements

Else statements can also be used in conjunction with **if** statements. Consider the following script segment.

```
if( a==5 )
{
  llSay(0,"a is equal to 5");
}
else
{
  llSay(0,"a is not equal to 5");
}
```

The **else** statement follows the **if** statement. If the **if** statement does not execute, the **else** statement will execute. It is illegal to have an **else** statement without a corresponding **if** statement. Unless some sort of error occurs, it is impossible to make it through an **if/else** statement without executing either the **if** statement's block of code, or the **else** statement's block of code.

It is also possible to use an **else if** statement. This is a combination of the **else** and **if** statements, as seen below.

```
if( a==5 )
{
  llSay(0,"a is equal to 5");
}
else if (a==6 )
{
  llSay(0,"a is equal to 6");
}
```

The above code contains two **if** statements. If **a** is not equal to five, then the second **if** statement is checked. If **a** is not equal to six, nothing happens. Any number of **if/else** statements can be strung together in this way. It is possible to create lengthy **if/else** ladders in this way. It is also possible to attach a final **else** statement to the ladder to execute if none of the above **if** statements executed. The following code demonstrates this.

```
if( a==1 )
{
  llSay(0,"a is equal to 1");
}
else if (a==2 )
{
  llSay(0,"a is equal to 2");
}
else if (a==3 )
{
  llSay(0,"a is equal to 3");
}
else
{
  llSay(0,"a is not equal to 1, 2 or 3");
}
```

The code above will execute one of the **if** statements if the variable is equal to one, two or three. The final **else** statement will be executed if none of the above three **if** statements match. The above technique is quite common in programming. Often the variable will be compared against a list of numbers.

No Support for Switch and Case

An **if/else** ladder can be used to compare a long list of numbers. Many languages include a special construct for this. The **switch** and **case** statements can also perform this task in many languages. The following script segment would compare the variable **a** against the numbers one, two and three.

```
switch( a )
{
  case 1:
    llSay(0,"a is equal to 1");
    break;
  case 2:
    llSay(0,"a is equal to 2");
    break;
  case 3:
```

```
    llSay(0,"a is equal to 3");
    break;
}
```

Unfortunatly the Linden Scripting Language does not currently support **switch** and **case**.

Using Loops

Loops allow a script to execute a block of code a certain number of times. Like many programming languages, the Linden Scripting Language supports three different types of loop. These loop types are summarized here.

- While Loops
- Do/While Loops
- For Loops

The next three sections will introduce these loop types.

While Loops

The most common loop type in the Linden Scripting Language is the **while** loop. A **while** statement looks very similar to an **if** statement. However, a **while** statement will execute the block of code as long as the specified expression is **true**. If the specified expression is not **true**, the **while** statement will not execute. It is important to note that a **while** statement can execute zero times. If the expression specified in the while is not **true** from the beginning, the **while** statement will not execute even once. The script shown in Listing 3.2 demonstrates a **while** loop.

Listing 3.2: A While Loop

```
default
{
    touch_start(integer total_number)
    {
        integer a = 1;

        while( a<=10 )
        {
            llSay(0, "Counting " + (string)a );
            a++;
        }
```

```
        }
}
```

The variable **a** is defined to hold the number one. The **while** loop begins by en-
suring that **a** is less than or equal to ten. If **a** is less than or equal to ten, the loop will
continue. The value of **a** is displayed and **a** is incremented. The loop continues.

It is also easy to count backwards in a loop. Simply reverse a few things and the
above loop will count backwards. This can be seen in Listing 3.3.

Listing 3.3: A While Loop Counts Backwards

```
default
{
    touch_start(integer total_number)
    {
        integer a = 10;

        while( a>=1 )
        {
            llSay(0, "Counting " + (string)a );
            a--;
        }
    }
}
```

Notice how the above loop now initializes the variable to 10. The **while** loop now
checks to be sure that the variable is still greater than one. Finally, each time through
the loop, the variable is decremented, as opposed to incremented.

Do/While Loops

If the expression is **false** from the beginning, the **while** loop cannot be guaranteed to execute. The do/while loop differs from the while loop in this very important
way. The **do/while** loop is guaranteed to execute at least once. This is because a
while loop makes its decision at the beginning of the loop. The **do/while** loop
makes this decision at the end of the loop. This can be seen in Listing 3.4.

Listing 3.4: A Do/While Loop

```
default
{
    touch_start(integer total_number)
    {
```

```
        integer a = 1;

        do
        {
            llSay(0, "Counting " + (string)a );
            a++;
        } while( a<=10 );
    }
}
```

In the above script, the variable is initialized to one. The **do/while** loop begins and displays the value of the variable. The variable is incremented. Next the **while**, at the end of the loop, checks to see whether the variable is still less than or equal to ten. If the variable is less than or equal to ten, the loop continues.

This loop performs the same task as the while loop in the previous section. You may be wondering why it matters to make the decision at the end. Consider the following script that illustrates this. Listing 3.5 illustrates this.

Listing 3.5: A Do/While Loop That Executes Once

```
default
{
    touch_start(integer total_number)
    {
        integer a = 20;

        do
        {
            llSay(0, "Counting " + (string)a );
            a++;
        } while( a<=10 );
    }
}
```

The above script sets the variable **a** to 20. This number is too high for the loop to use. The **while** loop from the previous section would simply fail to execute and nothing would be displayed. However, the above script is guaranteed to execute at least once. This would cause the above loop to simply display one line, the value 20.

For Loops

The third loop type, the **for** loop, can be very useful when you know the exact range that is to be looped over. For a simple loop to count between one and ten, the **for** loop is the loop of choice. Consider the following loop which counts between one and ten. Listing 3.6 illustrates this.

Listing 3.6: A For Loop

```
default
{
    touch_start(integer total_number)
    {
        integer a;

        for(a = 1; a<=10; a++ )
        {
            llSay(0, "Counting " + (string)a );
        }
    }
}
```

As can be seen from the above code, the for loop has three parts. The first part initializes the variable to one. The second, or middle part, of the **for** loop works like a **while** loop. As long as this expression is **true**, the loop will continue. The third, and final part of the **for** loop, is the action that should take place each iteration through the loop. For this simple loop, the variable is simply incremented.

Summary

Loops and control statements allow you to control the execution flow of the script. The **if** statements allow the script to make decisions and conditionally execute blocks of code. The **switch** and **case** statements work similarly to **if** statements except that they allow conditional execution based on a series of numeric values.

When a block of code should be executed repeatedly, a loop should be considered. The Linden Scripting Language supports three loop types. The **while** loop will only execute if the initial condition is true. A **do/while** loop will execute at least once. A **for** loop executes over a defined set of numbers.

All Second Life scripts are state machines. State machines are a common programming technique for organizing the execution of the program. The next chapter will explore state machines.

CHAPTER 4: STATE MACHINES

- What is a state machine?
- State machines in Second Life
- Using state machines
- Programming with and without state machines

The concept of a state machine is not unique to Second Life. State machines are a common programming paradigm. However, no language makes the concept of a state machine as integral as does the Linden Scripting Language. Most of the scripts in this book will be implemented as state machines.

This chapter begins by introducing the concept of a state machine. State machines will be introduced independent of Second Life. Next, this chapter will explain how Second Life implements state machines. Finally, this chapter will conclude by showing how to implement a script both with, and without, state machines.

What is a State Machine?

A state machine is a common way to represent a computer program. The computer program contains a finite number of states. The program will proceed from one state to the next through a series of actions. The program will begin in one specific state and may either eventually end, or continue running endlessly. Figure 4.1 shows a typical state engine.

Figure 4.1: A State Machine

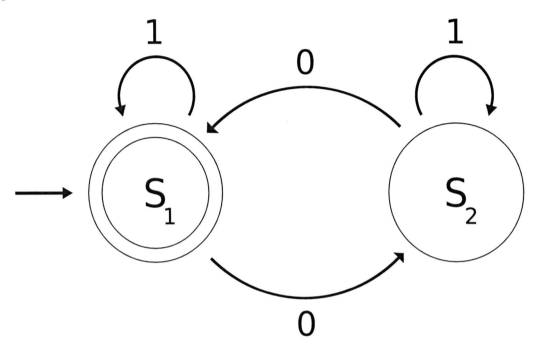

The above figure represents a state machine. Each of the circles represents an individual state. The arrows represent the actions that will take the script from one state to another. State machines always start in the specified starting state, which is called the accept state. The accept state is shown in Figure 4.1 as the state that is enclosed by a double line.

A state machine may end with some terminal state is reached. However, most Second Life scripts will continue executing indefinitely.

Understanding Second Life State Machines

To see state machines in action, consider the **default** script, which is automatically generated by Second Life, when a new script is created. This script is shown here.

```
default
{
    state_entry()
    {
        llSay(0, "Hello, Avatar!");
    }
```

```
    touch_start(integer total_number)
    {
        llSay(0,  "Touched.");
    }
}
```

This script starts with the word **default**. The word **default** specifies the name of the state that the enclosed code belongs to. For this script there is only one state. This state, which is named **default**, is the starting state for any script in Second Life.

Life With and Without State Machines

Many scripts are constructed entirely within their **default** state. This is often bad design in Second Life. Consider the following script, which implements a simple switch that can be turned on or off.

Listing 4.1: Programming without State Machines

```
integer value;

default
{
    state_entry()
    {
        value = TRUE;
    }

    touch_start(integer total_number)
    {
        if( value==TRUE )
        {
            llSay(0,"On");
            value = FALSE;
        }
        else
        {
            llSay(0,"Off");
            value = TRUE;
        }
    }
}
```

As can be seen, a global variable, named **value**, is set to either **TRUE** or **FALSE**. As the user touches the object, the object will say either "On" or "Off". As the object is touched these values will alternate. Also, a note on global variables. Global variables are normally considered bad programming practice. However in Second Life, there is really little choice as to whether to use them or not. Because the Linden Scripting Language does not support user defined classes, global variables are the primary way for a script to hold values long-term.

This same functionality could be created using a state machine. The following lines of code do this.

Listing 4.2: Programming with State Machines

```
default
{
    touch_start(integer total_number)
    {
        llSay(0,"On");
        state off;
    }
}

state off
{
    touch_start(integer total_number)
    {
        llSay(0,"Off");
        state default;
    }
}
```

The above code creates a second state, named **off**. This gives the above script two states: **default** and **off**. Both states contain their own **touch_start** event. Both states also use the **state** command to switch to the opposite state when the object is touched. To create an additional state use the **state** statement followed by the name of the new state. This was done in the above script with the **off** state.

This script, like all scripts, begins in the **default** state. To leave the **default** state and enter another state, use the **state** statement. For example, the following command will switch to the **off** state:

```
state off;
```

As can be seen in the above script, the **state** statement is used in the **touch_start** event to switch to the off state. Likewise, the **touch_start** in the **off** state switches the state back to **default**.

Whenever a state is entered, the **state_entry** event is called. This allows the script to setup for the new state. The above script does not make use of a **state_entry** event. However, **state_entry** events could have been added for both the **default** and **off** states. The **state_entry** event for a **default** state is often used to setup the script, as can be seen in the following script.

Listing 4.3: State events

```
default
{
    state_entry()
    {
        llSay(0,
"The script has entered the default state.");
    }

    touch_start(integer total_number)
    {
        state mystate;
    }
}

state mystate
{
    state_entry()
    {
        llSay(0,
"The script has entered the mystate state.");
    }

    touch_start(integer total_number)
    {
        state default;
    }
}
```

The above script will cycle through two states. When each state is entered, the **state_entry** event will be called. This could be used to setup any script variables needed by the state. In this example, the **state_entry** event simply displays the name of the state that has been entered.

It is invalid to declare "state level" variables. For example, the following script segment would be invalid.

```
state mystate
{
    string stringForMyState;
```

```
state_entry()
{
}

touch_start(integer total_number)
{
}
}
```

The above script segment is attempting to declare the variable **stringForMyState** inside of the state **mystate**. This is not allowed. Such a variable should be declared at the top of the script. This will cause the variable to be accessible from anywhere in the script. It is not possible to create variables that are only accessible inside a particular state. Variables are either accessible from the entire script, or they are accessible from inside of the function that declared them.

If you are not used to using state engines it may seem unnatural to use them. It is not required that your scripts make use of state engines. As explained earlier in this chapter it is possible to create scripts without making use of state engines. However, the Linden Scripting Language is optimized for state engines. Because of this, state engines should be used when possible.

Summary

State machines are an inherent part of the Linden Scripting Language. A Second Life script moves through a series of states as it executes. All scripts begin execution in the default state. As the script executes, it can move to other states by using the state command.

Strings allow the script to manipulate textual information. Strings have been used by many of the programs demonstrated so far. The next chapter will take an in depth look at strings. The functions used to parse and manipulate strings will be covered.

CHAPTER 5: STRING HANDLING

- Comparing strings
- Determining string set membership
- Parsing strings
- Reading notecards

Strings are sequences of characters. These strings usually come from a note-card, are spoken by an avatar, or by the script itself. Declaring a string in the Linden Scripting Language is very easy. The following lines of code create a string named **myString** that contains the text "Hello World".

```
string myString = "Hello World";
```

First, **string** comparison functions will be demonstrated. These functions will allow the script to compare strings in a variety of ways. Finally, **string** parsing will be demonstrated.

String Functions

The Linden Scripting Language offers several functions to perform core **string** operations. While the list of **string** functions for the Linden Scripting Language is not extensive, they do provide functions to perform all of the fundamental string operations. Table 5.1 summarizes the string functions offered by the Linden Scripting Language.

Table 5.1: Linden String Functions

Function	Purpose
llDeleteSubString	removes a slice of a string.
llDumpList2String	turns a list into a string.
llParseString2List	turns a string into a list.
llParseStringKeepNulls	turns a string into a list, keep nulls.
llGetSubString	extracts a part of a string.
llInsertString	inserts a string into a string.
llToLower	converts a string to lowercase.
llToUpper	converts a string to UPPERCASE.
llStringTrim	removes leading and/or trailing spaces.

llStringLength	gets the length of a string.
llSubStringIndex	finds the position of a string in another string.
llEscapeURL	returns the string that is the URL-escaped version of url. (replacing spaces with %20, etc).
llUnescapeURL	returns the string that is the URL unescaped version of url, replacing "%20" with spaces, etc.

Many of these functions will be explained in this chapter.

String Comparison

The Linden Scripting Language makes it very easy to compare two strings. To compare two strings, named **stra** and **strb**, the following code would normally be used:

```
if( stra == strb )
{
   llSay(0,"Equal.");
}
```

While this method of string comparison is good for determining whether two strings are exactly equal to each other, sometimes more advanced string comparison is called for. A script might need to determine whether two strings are equal, and ignore the case. Additionally, it might be necessary to determine which string would appear first in a dictionary.

Listing 5.1 meets these needs.

Listing 5.1: String Comparison

```
string CHARS = "!\"#$%&'()*+,-./0123456789:;<=>?@ABCDEFGHIJKLMNOP
QRSTUVWXYZ[\]^_`abcdefghijklmnopqrstuvwxyz{|}~";


integer compareLen(string a, string b,integer len)
{
    integer result = 0;
    if(a != b)
    {
        integer index = 0;
        do
        {
            string chara = llGetSubString(a,index,index);
            string charb = llGetSubString(b,index,index);

            integer posa = llSubStringIndex(CHARS ,chara);
```

```
            integer posb = llSubStringIndex(CHARS ,charb);

            if((posa >= 0) && (posb >= 0))
            {
                result = posa - posb;
            }
            else if(posa >= 0)
            {
                result = 1;
            }
            else if(posb >= 0)
            {
                result = -1;
            }

            if(result != 0) index = len;
            ++index;

        }
        while(index < len);
    }

    return result;
}

integer compareNoCaseLen(string a, string b,integer len)
{
    string stra = llToLower(a);
    string strb = llToLower(b);
    return compareLen(stra,strb,len);
}

integer compare(string a, string b)
{
    integer lena = llStringLength(a);
    integer lenb = llStringLength(b);
    integer result;
    if(lena < lenb)
        result =  compareLen(a,b,lena);
    else
        result =  compareLen(a,b,lenb);

    return result;
}


integer compareNoCase(string a, string b)
```

```
{
    integer la = llStringLength(a);
    integer lb = llStringLength(b);
    string stra = llToLower(a);
    string strb = llToLower(b);
    integer result;
    if(la < lb)
        result =  compareNoCaseLen(stra,strb,la);
    else
        result =  compareNoCaseLen(stra,strb,lb);

    return result;
}

// Some test uses
default
{
    state_entry()
    {
        llSay(0, "compareNoCase(hello,HELLO): " +
            (string)compareNoCase("jeff","Jeff") );
        llSay(0, "compare(hello,HELLO): " +
            (string)compare("jeff","Jeff") );
        llSay(0, "compare(aaa,bbb): " +
            (string)compare("aaa","bbb") );
        llSay(0, "compare(aaa,bbb): " +
            (string)compare("bbb","aaa") );

    }
}
```

This listing begins by defining a variable, named **CHARS**, that holds all of the characters that can be compared. This variable, also defines the order that characters will be sorted in. This variable is declared as follows:

```
string CHARS = "!\"#$%&'()*+,-./0123456789:;<=>?@ABCDEFGHIJKLMNOP
QRSTUVWXYZ[\]^_`abcdefghijklmnopqrstuvwxyz{|}~";
```

For example, if the character "!" were compared to "#", the string comparison function would report that "!" occurs first, and "#" second. This is because of the order of these two characters in the above list.

Using the compareLen Function

To compare two strings, the **compareLen** function is provided.

```
integer compareLen(string a,  string b,integer len)
{
```

The **compareLen** function accepts three parameters. The first two are the strings to compare. The third parameter is the length of characters to compare. For example, if five were specified as the **len** variable, characters zero through four would be compared.

The **compareLen** function will return one of the following three values.

- Less than zero, string **a** is less than string **b**
- Zero, string **a** and string **b** are equal
- Greater than zero, string **a** is greater than string **b**

A variable, named **result** is created to hold the **result** of the comparison. If the two strings are not equal, the program begins the process of determining which **string** will occur first alphabetically.

```
integer result = 0;
if(a != b)
{
    integer index = 0;
    do
    {
```

To determine which **string** occurs first alphabetically, a **do/loop** is used to loop across all of the characters in the **string**.

```
string chara = llGetSubString(a,index,index);
string charb = llGetSubString(b,index,index);
```

The individual characters for each position are extracted from the strings.

```
integer posa = llSubStringIndex(CHARS ,chara);
integer posb = llSubStringIndex(CHARS ,charb);
```

The position of each character is calculated. This numeric value allows the program to determine the alphabetical order of the two characters.

If both **posa** and **posb** are greater than zero, both characters were found in the **CHARS** variable. If this is the case, the **result** will simply be the difference between them. If they are equal, this will result in a value of zero. If they are not equal, **result** will hold a value either greater or less than zero, depending on whether **posa** or **posb** was greater.

```
if((posa >= 0) && (posb >= 0))
{
    result = posa - posb;
}
```

If character **a** was found, but not character **b**, return a value of one, which indicates that string **a** is greater than string **b**.

```
          else if(posa >= 0)
          {
               result = 1;
          }
```

If character **b** was found, but not character **a**, return a value of negative one, which indicates that string **b** is greater than string **a**.

```
          else if(posb >= 0)
          {
               result = -1;
          }
```

If the two characters were equal, continue with the loop.

```
          if(result != 0) index = len;
          ++index;
```

Continue looping until the end of the string is reached.

```
        }
      while(index < len);
   }
   return result;
}
```

Finally, return the **result**.

Understanding the compareNoCaseLen Function

Sometimes it is useful to compare two strings and ignore case. The **compareNoCaseLen** function does this. The **compareNoCaseLen** function accepts three parameters. The first two are the strings to compare. The third parameter is the length of characters to compare.

```
integer compareNoCaseLen(string a, string b,integer len)
{
```

First, the two strings are converted to lower case.

```
   string stra = llToLower(a);
   string strb = llToLower(b);
   return compareLen(stra,strb,len);
}
```

Finally, they are compared using the **compareLen** function discussed in the previous section.

Understanding the compare Function

The two string functions presented so far allow a length to be specified. This can be very useful if only the first part of the strings should be compared. However, usually the entire string should be compared. The **compare** function will compare the entire string.

```
integer compare(string a, string b)
{
```

First, the length of each string is calculated.

```
    integer lena = llStringLength(a);
    integer lenb = llStringLength(b);
```

The **compareLen** method is called to perform the actual comparison. The length of the smallest string will be used in the comparison.

```
    integer result;
    if(lena < lenb)
        result =  compareLen(a,b,lena);
    else
        result =  compareLen(a,b,lenb);

    return result;
}
```

Finally, the **result** is returned.

Understanding the compareNoCase Function

The **compareNoCase** function works just like **compareNoCaseLen**, except that no length is provided. The entire string will be compared.

```
integer compareNoCase(string a, string b)
{
```

First the **length** of each **string** is calculated.

```
    integer la = llStringLength(a);
    integer lb = llStringLength(b);
```

Next, the strings are converted into lowercase.

```
    string stra = llToLower(a);
    string strb = llToLower(b);
    integer result;
```

The **compareLen** method is called to perform the actual comparison. The length of the smallest string will be used in the comparison.

```
    if(la < lb)
```

```
        result =  compareLen(stra,strb,la);
    else
        result =  compareLen(stra,strb,lb);

    return result;
}
```

Finally, the **result** is returned.

Comparing Strings

The script includes a simple **state_entry** function that tests the functions presented in this script.

```
default
{
    state_entry()
    {
        llSay(0, "compareNoCase(hello,HELLO): " +
            (string)compareNoCase("jeff","Jeff") );
        llSay(0, "compare(hello,HELLO): " +
            (string)compare("jeff","Jeff") );
        llSay(0, "compare(aaa,bbb): " +
            (string)compare("aaa","bbb") );
        llSay(0, "compare(aaa,bbb): " +
            (string)compare("bbb","aaa") );
    }
}
```

The output from this script is shown here.

```
[20:52]  Object: compareNoCase(hello,HELLO): 0
[20:52]  Object: compare(hello,HELLO): 31
[20:52]  Object: compare(aaa,bbb): -1
[20:52]  Object: compare(aaa,bbb): 1
```

The above output demonstrates how the functions, created earlier in this chapter, can be used.

Using Notecards

Notecards can be a handy way to store **string** based information for a script to use. Notecards are an object type that can be embedded inside of any Second Life object. A note is nothing more than a collection of text. Very similar to a text file stored on your hard drive.

Scripts can easily read from notecards that are stored in the same object as the script. However, scripts cannot write to notecards. Notecards are very easy to modify. The owner of an object can simply open the contents of a object that contains a note-card. Notecards must be created in your inventory. To create a notecard open your inventory and select the notecards folder. You can right-click the notecards folder and select "New Notecard". This will create the notecard in your inventory, as seen in Figure 5.1.

Figure 5.1: Creating a Notecard

There are many notecards in my inventory, as seen in Figure 5.1. The new notecard is named "New Note". The notecard can now be drug to your object and renamed.

This notecard can be seen in Listing 5.2.

Listing 5.2: A Simple Notecard

```
Item 1:This is configuration item 1
```

```
Item 2:This is configuration item 2
Item 3:This is configuration item 3
```

The above notecard is a simple configuration file. There are three configuration items. The first is named "Item 1". The script, that will be presented to read this configuration file, will look for each of these configuration and parse the data contained after the configuration item.

A script can easily read notecards by using the appropriate Linden Scripting Language functions. Listing 5.3 shows such a script.

Listing 5.3: Reading Notecards

```
integer index;
string notecardName;
key notecardQuery;
integer notecardIndex;
integer loaded = FALSE;

string item1;
string item2;
string item3;

default
{
    state_entry()
    {
        if( loaded == FALSE )
        {
            notecardName = "Config";
            state loading;
        }
        else
        {
            index = 0;
            llSay(0,"Config data:");
            llSay(0,"Item 1's value: " + item1);
            llSay(0,"Item 2's value: " + item2);
            llSay(0,"Item 3's value: " + item3);
        }
    }


}


state loading
{
```

```
state_entry()
{
    llSay(0,"Loading configuration data...");
    notecardIndex = 0;
    notecardQuery = llGetNotecardLine(notecardName,
        notecardIndex++);
}


dataserver(key query_id, string data)
{
    if ( notecardQuery == query_id)
    {
        // this is a line of our notecard
        if (data == EOF)
        {
            llSay(0,"Config loaded...");
            loaded = TRUE;
            state default;

        } else
        {
            integer i = llSubStringIndex(data, ":");
            if( i!=-1 )
            {
                string name = llGetSubString(data,0,i-1);
                string value = llGetSubString(data,i+1,-1);

                if( name=="Item 1" )
                {
                    item1 = value;
                }
                else if( name=="Item 2" )
                    item2 = value;
                if( name=="Item 3" )
                    item3 = value;
            }

            notecardQuery = llGetNotecardLine(notecardName,
              notecardIndex++);
        }
    }
}
```

This script begins by defining several script level variables. These variables will be accessible from any of the states that the script may find itself in.

```
integer index;
string notecardName;
key notecardQuery;
integer notecardIndex;
integer loaded = FALSE;
```

The **notecardIndex** variable holds the current notecard line being read. The **notecardName** variable holds the name of the notecard to read. The **notecardQuery** variable holds the query being used to read the notecard. The **loaded** variable holds a boolean to determine whether the notecard has been read yet.

Each of the configuration items will be stored in strings named **item1**, **item2** and **item3**. These variables could be replaced with any configuration items that you are modifying this script to be able to parse.

```
string item1;
string item2;
string item3;
```

The notecard script, as do all scripts, begins in the **default** state. The state begins by checking the **loaded** variable. If the notecard has not yet been read, the script enters the **loading** state.

```
default
{
    state_entry()
    {
        if( loaded == FALSE )
        {
            notecardName = "Config";
            state loading;
        }
```

If the notecard has already been loaded, display the item data.

```
        else
        {
            index = 0;
            llSay(0,"Config data:");
            llSay(0,"Item 1's value: " + item1);
            llSay(0,"Item 2's value: " + item2);
            llSay(0,"Item 3's value: " + item3);
        }
    }
}
```

The **loading** state is where the notecard is actually read. First, the **notecardIndex** variable is set to zero. This will begin reading the notecard at the first line. Next **llGetNotecardLine** is called to read the first line from the notecard. The **llGetNotecardLine** does not return the line immediately. Rather the **dataserver** event will be called as soon as the line is read.

```
state loading
{
    state_entry()
    {
        llSay(0,"Loading configuration data...");
        notecardIndex = 0;
        notecardQuery = llGetNotecardLine(notecardName,notecardIndex++);
    }
}
```

As the lines are read in from the notecard, the **dataserver** event is called. If the **query_id** matches our notecard query established earlier, this is a line that should be processed.

```
    dataserver(key query_id, string data)
    {
        if ( notecardQuery == query_id)
        {
```

If this line is from our query, check to see whether it is an end-of-file (**EOF**). If the file has ended, set the **loaded** variable to **TRUE** and return to the **default** state.

```
            // this is a line of our notecard
            if (data == EOF)
            {
                llSay(0,"Config loaded...");
                loaded = TRUE;
                state default;

            } else
            {
```

If the line is part of the notecard, and not an end-of-file, we must determine which configuration item was just read. Configuration items begin with the name of the item, followed by a colon. The first step is to find the location of the colon. The following line of code does this.

```
            integer i = llSubStringIndex(data, ":");
```

The variable **i** now contains the location of the first colon encountered. If no colon was encountered then the value -1 is returned.

```
            if( i!=-1 )
```

```
        {
```

The name of the configuration item comes just before the colon. The name is then extracted into the name variable. The name occurs between position zero and one minus the position that ht colon was found at.

```
string name = llGetSubString(data,0,i-1);
```

The value occurs to the right of the colon. The value is extracted by obtaining all characters from one plus the colon to the end of the string. The value of -1 can be passed to **llGetSubString** to obtain the end of the string.

```
string value = llGetSubString(data,i+1,-1);
```

Now that both the name and value have been obtained it is time to see which configuration item was specified. The next few lines determine which configuration item was specified and copy the value to the appropriate script variable.

```
if( name=="Item 1" )
{
    item1 = value;
}
else if( name=="Item 2" )
    item2 = value;
if( name=="Item 3" )
    item3 = value;
}
```

Next, the next line of the notecard is read.

```
notecardQuery = llGetNotecardLine(notecardName,
    notecardIndex++);
        }
    }
  }
}
```

This process will continue until all lines have been read from the notecard.

Summary

A **string** is a set of characters. Strings are usually received from other avatars or notecards. Strings are how the Linden Scripting Language represents text. The Linden Scripting Language provides many built in functions to handle strings.

Strings can be read from notecards. A notecard is essentially a file that is attached to an object. Notecards are commonly used to hold configuration information for scripts. Strings read in from notecards are usually parsed to obtain the configuration information.

So far our scripts have performed basic communication. These scripts "say" things to the world around then. Scripts can also listen and send instant messages, as well as other forms of communication. Communication will be covered in the next chapter.

CHAPTER **6**: COMMUNICATION

- Speaking, Whispering and Shouting
- Region-wide Communicate
- Using Dialogs
- Instant Messages
- Linked Messages

There are many ways to communicate in Second Life. Objects can communicate with avatars in many of the same ways that avatars communicate with each other. Objects can also use special communications channels to communicate with each other. Additionally, dialogs can be presented to users to allow them to pick from several options.

Instant messages (IM) are another common way for avatars to communicate with each other. Objects can also communicate via instant message. An object can send an instant message to an avatar. However, it is currently impossible, in the Linden Scripting Language, to send an instant message from an object. This includes both IMs from other objects, as well as IMs from avatars.

This chapter will explain how objects can communicate. It will explain both communication between objects and avatars, as well as communication between objects.

Speaking and Listening

Spoken communication in Second Life occurs over channels. When avatars converse with each other, they are communicating on channel 0. Anything that is said on channel 0 near an avatar will be displayed to the screen. Figure 6.1 shows an avatar hearing communication around him.

Figure 6.1: Conversation on Channel 0

Messages on other channels are not displayed to avatars. These other channels are reserved for objects and there is no easy way for an avatar to listen on one of these channels. However, avatars can easily talk on other channels. By prefixing what the avatar is saying with a slash, and then a number, the avatar can speak on other channels. For example, the following would say "Hello" on channel 1.

```
/1Hello
```

Many objects use this as a means of receiving commands from the object's owner. The object could have just as easily accepted a command on channel 0; however, by accepting it over channel 1, the command will not be broadcast to other nearby avatars.

Objects in Second Life can communicate in many of the same ways that avatars communicate. Objects can listen to conversations going on around them. Objects can also speak and participate in those conversations. Objects can also send instant messages to avatars. However, instant messages between an avatar and an object are one-way. An avatar cannot send an instant message back to an object.

The following script demonstrates how an object can listen to conversations going on around it. The object will wait for someone to say either "hello" or "goodbye". Once the object detects either of these words, the object says an appropriate greeting to the avatar that spoke to the object. This can be seen in Listing 6.1.

Listing 6.1: Say Hello

```
integer CHANNEL = 0;

default
{
    state_entry()
    {
        llListen(CHANNEL, "", NULL_KEY, "");
    }

    listen(integer channel, string name, key id,
      string message)
    {
        if( llToLower(message) == "hello" )
        {
            llSay(CHANNEL,"Hello " + name );
        }
        else if( llToLower(message) == "goodbye" )
        {
            llSay(CHANNEL,"Goodbye " + name );
        }
    }
}
```

For an object to begin listening, the object must call the **llListen** function. This function specifies what channel the object would like to listen on. The above script calls the **llListen** function in the **state_entry** event handler. The script specifies that it would like to listen to the channel specified by the **CHANNEL** variable. The Linden Scripting Language does not have user defined constants. As a result, the above declaration of **CHANNEL** is as close as we can come to a constant.

Channel zero is the normal conversation channel in Second Life. All communication between avatars is on channel zero. Therefore, by requesting to listen on channel zero, the object will be notified anytime something is said near to the object.

The above script contains a **listen** event handler. This event handler is called each time something is said near the object. The object checks for either "hello" or "goodbye". Because the strings are converted to lower case, the user could also enter "Hello" or any mixture of upper and lower case characters. The script responds with a greeting directed to the avatar's name. The avatar's name was passed in as a parameter named **name**.

The **llSay** function is used when a script wants to say something. The above calls to **llSay** use channel zero. However, objects will often want to communicate with each other, and not allow nearby avatars to listen in. To do this, the script should specify a channel other than zero. Many recipes in this book will communicate on channels other than zero.

In addition to **llSay**, there are two other functions that allow a script to talk. The only difference between the three communication functions is the distance they cover. Table 6.1 summarizes the communication functions.

Table 6.1: Communication Distances

Communication Function	Distance
llWhisper	10m
llSay	20m
llShout	100m

There is also a fourth communication function, that has unlimited range. The **llInstantMessage** function allows an instant message to be sent to the specified avatar. This can be seen in Listing 6.2.

Listing 6.2: Instant Message

```
default
{
    touch_start(integer total_num)
    {
      // get the key of the objects owner.
      key owner=llGetOwner();
        llInstantMessage(owner,llKey2Name(owner)+", "
        + (string)total_num +" Avatar(s) touched me!");
    }
}
```

The above script will send a message to the object's owner every time the object is touched. It is also possible to send a message to the object's owner by using the **llOwnerSay** function. However, **llOwnerSay** does not have the unlimited distance of a **llInstantMessage** function call.

It is also possible to communicate to the entire region. The command **llRegionSay** will send a message to objects across the entire region. The **llRegionSay** function cannot be used on channel 0. Therefore, **llRegionSay** is only useful for communications between objects.

Understanding Dialogs

The Linden Scripting Language allows much more direct interaction with avatars than simple touch events. It is also possible to create a dialog. A Second Life dialog can be seen in Figure 6.2.

Figure 6.2: Second Life Dialogs

The dialog allows the user to select a color. This script used to do this can be seen in Listing 6.3.

Listing 6.3: A Second Life Dialog

```
integer CHANNEL = 10;

default
{
    state_entry()
    {
        llListen(CHANNEL, "", NULL_KEY, "");
    }
```

```
touch_start(integer total_num)
{
    list l = ["red","green","blue"];
    key who = llDetectedKey(0);
    llDialog(who, "Where to?", l, CHANNEL);
}

listen(integer channel, string name, key id,
  string message)
{
    if( llToLower(message) == "red" )
    {
        llSetColor(<255,0,0>,ALL_SIDES);
    }
    else if( llToLower(message) == "green" )
    {
        llSetColor(<0,255,0>,ALL_SIDES);
    }
    else if( llToLower(message) == "blue" )
    {
        llSetColor(<0,0,255>,ALL_SIDES);
    }
}
}
```

This script is very similar to the script presented in the last section. There are two main differences. First, this script makes use of channel 10, rather than channel zero. The second difference is that this script makes use of a dialog.

The dialog is used at the end of the **touch_start** event handler. Calling the **llDialog** function creates a dialog. The dialog will display buttons that correspond to the **list** that was passed into the **llDialog** function.

Once the user selects one of the options from the dialog, the name of that button is "said" over the specified channel. This causes the user's choice to be picked up by the **listen** event handler. In this way, implementing a dialog is very similar to implementing a script that listens to user conversation.

Instant Messages

Objects can send instant messages directly to an avatar. It is currently impossible for objects to receive instant messages, either from avatars or other objects. Instant messages are sent using the **llInstantMessage** function. However, there is a shortcut for sending an instant message to the owner of an object. To send an instant message to the owner of an object, the **llOwnerSay** function should be used.

However, to send an instant message to someone other than the owner, the **llInstantMessage** function must be used. Listing 6.4 shows a simple pager that uses **llInstantMessage**.

Listing 6.4: A Simple Pager

```
string name = "";
string last_online = "";
key nameKey = NULL_KEY;

default
{
    on_rez(integer p)
    {
        llResetScript();
    }

    state_entry()
    {
        llSetText("Online Detector\nTouch to Claim",<1,1,1>,1);
    }

    touch_start(integer total_number)
    {
        if(name == "")
        {
            nameKey = llDetectedKey(0);
            name = llDetectedName(0);
            llSetText(name + "\Touch to page:\n" +
                    name,<1,1,1>,1);
        }
        else if(llDetectedName(0) != name)
        {
            llInstantMessage(nameKey, llDetectedName(0) +
            " is paging you from " + llGetRegionName());
            llWhisper(0,"A message has been sent to " + name);
        }
    }
}
```

The script begins by defining several script level variables. Specifically, the name and the **key** for the user, who has claimed the pager, are stored. A **key** is a number that represents an object or avatar in Second Life. The **key** will be obtained when an avatar touches the pager. The first avatar to touch the pager claims that pager and will be sent instant messages when others touch it.

```
string name = "";
```

```
key nameKey = NULL_KEY;
```

This script has one single state, the **default** state, that all scripts have.

```
default
{
```

Because the object is claimed, it should be reset whenever it is rezzed back to the world. Thus, if an avatar who has claimed this object gives the object to a second avatar, the object will go unclaimed as soon as it is moved back to the world from the user's inventory.

```
on_rez(integer p)
{
    llResetScript();
}
```

When the object first starts up, text is displayed above the object instructing avatars to touch the object to claim it.

```
state_entry()
{
    llSetText("Online Detector\nTouch to Claim",<1,1,1>,1);
}
```

If an avatar touches the pager, then either that avatar is going to send a message or claim the pager. If no one has claimed the pager yet, the touching avatar claims it. If it is to be claimed then use **llDetectedKey** and **llDetectedName** to obtain the name of the avatar who has claimed the pager. These functions return the name and **key** of the avatar that touched the object.

```
touch_start(integer total_number)
{
    if(name == "")
    {
        nameKey = llDetectedKey(0);
        name = llDetectedName(0);
        llSetText(name + "\Touch to page:\n"
                + name,<1,1,1>,1);
    }
```

If the pager was already claimed, send a message to the pager's owner to tell them that they were paged. Also include the region name where the pager was located.

```
    else if(llDetectedName(0) != name)
    {
        llInstantMessage(nameKey, llDetectedName(0)
        + " is paging you from " + llGetRegionName());
        llWhisper(0,"A message has been sent to " + name);
    }
}
```

}

It is possible for two avatars to touch the object at exactly the same instant. This is a rare occurrence and most scripts in Second Life do not support it. If two avatars did touch the object at exactly the same instance, the **total_number** parameter to the **touch** event would be greater than one. To support this, **llDetectedName** and **llInstantMessage** functions both accept a parameter to specify which avatar should be detected. The script above only supports one avatar touching the script at once, so a zero is passed in.

Supporting more than one avatar is relatively easy. Loop up to the number specified by **total_number** and process each avatar by calling a function such as **llDetectedName** for each. Of course, this does not always make sense for a script. The above script can only be claimed by one avatar at once. As a result, concurrent touches are not supported.

Setting Prim Text

Every prim has text associated with it. For most prims this text is an empty string (""). However, by using the **llSetText** function call, text can be assigned to a prim. This text will be displayed just above the prim, as seen in Figure 6.3.

Figure 6.3: Prim Text

The **llSetText** function has the following signature.

```
llSetText(string text, vector color, float alpha)
```

The first parameter, named **text**, specifies the text to be displayed. The second parameter, named **color**, specifies the color that the text is to be displayed in. Colors in Second Life are implemented using the **vector** data type. Colors are made up of red, green and blue components. These are mapped to the x, y and z-coordinates of the vector. The final parameter, named **alpha**, specifies the transparency of the text. A value of zero is completely transparent, whereas a value of one is completely solid.

Once a call to **llSetText** has been placed, the text will remain until it is cleared. To clear text the following function call is used.

```
llSetText("",<0,0,0>,0);
```

The following function call would display "Hello" in bright red.

```
llSetText("Hello.", <1,0,0>, 1.0);
```

The text property of a primitive provides a quick means to communicate textual information to all avatars around the prim.

Linked Messages

Second Life objects are made of a series of linked prims. These linked prims will move as one single object. The most important of the linked prims is the root prim. The root prim is the last prim that was linked to the object. Additionally, the root prim is the prim that translates its movement and rotation to the rest of the object. The root prim can be thought of as the "handle" by which the rest of the object is moved and rotated. The main script for an object is almost always located in the root prim.

Sometimes the linked prims in an object will need to communicate with each other. While these objects could certainly use **llSay** and **listen** events, this would not be the most efficient way to program this. Using **llSay** would broadcast the message well beyond the object that needs the communication. This would be very inefficient and would consume entirely too much processing time from the regional server. The best way to communicate among linked prims is to use linked messages.

A simple linked object is shown in Figure 6.4.

Figure 6.4: A Simple Linked Object

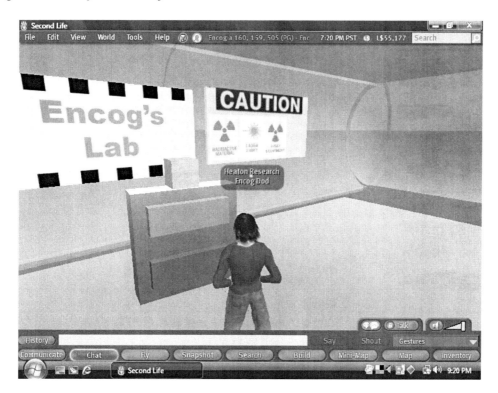

The above object contains two buttons, a red one and a green one. The cube at the top of the object changes colors depending on which button is clicked. When the buttons are touched, they send a message to the cube at the top. The green button's script is very short, and contains only a touch event. The green button's script can be seen in Listing 6.5.

Listing 6.5: The Green Button

```
default
{
    touch_start(integer total_number)
    {
        llMessageLinked(LINK_ROOT , 0, "Green", NULL_KEY);
    }
}
```

The red button is very similar to the green button. The red button can be seen in Listing 6.6.

Listing 6.6: The Red Button

```
default
{
    touch_start(integer total_number)
    {
        llMessageLinked(LINK_ROOT , 0, "Red", NULL_KEY);
    }
}
```

You will notice that the first parameter specifies which prims to send the message to. The value of **LINK_ROOT** sends the message to the root prim. There are several other options, as seen in Table 6.2.

Table 6.2: Message Target Types

Type	Purpose
LINK_ROOT	Send a message to the root prim.
LINK_SET	Send a message to all prims.
LINK_ALL_OTHERS	Send a message to all prims, except the one that contains this script.
LINK_ALL_CHILDREN	Send a message to all non-root prims.

LINK_THIS	Send a message to the prim that contains the script.

The remaining three parameters to the **llMessageLinked** function are sent on to the prims that receive the message. They can be used however you like. They allow an **integer**, a **string** and a **key** to all be sent to the receiving prim.

The root prim for this object is the box at the top that changes colors as the buttons are pressed. The script for the root prim is shown in Listing 6.7.

Listing 6.7: The Root Prim that Receives the Messages

```
default
{
    link_message(integer sender_num, integer num, string str, key
id)
    {
        llSay(0,"Message from " + (string) sender_num );
        if( str=="Red" )
        {
            llSetColor(<1,0,0>,ALL_SIDES);
        }
        else if( str=="Green" )
        {
            llSetColor(<0,1,0>,ALL_SIDES);
        }
    }
}
```

As you can see a **link_message** event handler is implemented. It receives messages from the two buttons. Depending on which button is pressed, the color of the cube is changed.

Summary

There are a variety of communication types that can be used in Second Life. Scripts can communicate both with other scripts and with avatars around them. Scripts can communicate on channel zero. Channel zero is the general chat channel that avatars use to converse. Scripts can both speak and listen on channel zero.

Scripts can also communicate on channels other than zero. This works the same as channel zero, except that avatars around the script will not be able to hear the conversation. Scripts can also send instant messages to avatars; however, a script may not receive instant messages.

Second Life objects are a collection of linked prims. Each of these linked prims can contain a script. These scripts can communicate with linked messages. A linked message is used to communicate between prims that are linked together.

Up to this point you have seen many examples of events. Events are special functions that are called by Second Life when something happens. The next chapter will focus on events and demonstrate many of their uses.

CHAPTER 7: EVENTS

- Timer Events
- Collision Events
- Sensor Events
- Money Events
- Using Dialogs

Events are very important to Second Life programming. Events have been used in many of the examples in previous chapters. This chapter will focus on some of the remaining event types that were not covered in previous chapters.

Events are functions, with a special name. The name of the event function defines the type of event that is to be handled. The event function will be called whenever that event occurs. This allows the script to respond to that event. So far we have seen touch and listen events. These events allow the script to hear messages around it and also detect when the object is touched. However, there are many other event types. In this chapter you will see how events can provide the following information:

- when a certain amount of time elapses
- when something collides with the object
- when other avatars are near the object
- when avatars pay money

Timer events will be discussed in the next section.

Timer Events

Perhaps the simplest kind of event is the **timer** event. Timer events happen periodically, according to the interval specified by a call to **llSetTimerEvent**. This can be seen in Listing 7.1.

Listing 7.1: Timer Events

```
default
{
    state_entry()
    {
        llSetTimerEvent(10);
    }

    timer()
    {
```

```
        llSay(0, "Timer");
    }
}
```

As can be seen above, timer is started in the **state_entry** event with a call to **llSetTimerEvent**. Once **llSetTimerEvent** has been called, the **timer** event will then be called at the interval specified by the **llSetTimerEvent** call. To disable the timer, call **llSetTimerEvent** with a value of zero.

Timers are very common in Second Life programming. Timers can be used anytime that it is necessary for a script to perform a repetitive task.

Collision Events

Collision events allow the script to determine when the object has collided with another object or the ground. There are three events that track collisions are named as follows.

- collision
- collision_end
- collision_start

The **collision_start** event is called when something first collides with the object. This could be an object or another avatar. Collisions with the ground are handled with the **land_collision** set of events that will be discussed next. All of the object collision events share a common signature.

```
collision( integer num_detected ){ ; }
collision_end( integer num_detected ){ ; }
collision_start( integer num_detected ){ ; }
```

When a collision is first detected, the **collision_start** event is sent. Next **collision** events are sent while the collision continues. Finally a **collision_end** event is sent when the collision stops.

The land collision functions work similarly. The three land collision events are listed here.

- land_collision
- land_collision_end
- land_collision_start

As you can see, the land collision events parallel the object collision events. However, there are differences. Land collisions do not involve multiple objects. The function signatures reflect that. The land collision events all share a similar signature. These signatures are shown here.

```
land_collision( vector pos ){ ; }
land_collision_start( vector pos ){ ; }
```

```
land_collision_end( vector pos ){ ; }
```

When a collision with the land is first detected, the **land_collision_start** event is sent. Next **land_collision** events are sent while the collision continues. Finally, a **land_collision_end** event is sent when the collision stops. Land collisions are only useful for physical objects. Physical objects are discussed in Chapter 10. Objects in Second Life are either physical or non-physical. A physical object can be moved by external forces, and will fall with gravity.

Listing 7.2 shows a simple collision script that shows how collisions work.

Listing 7.2: Working with Collisions

```
default
{

    collision(integer total_number)
    {
        integer i;
        for(i=0;i<total_number;i++)
        {
            llSay(0, "Collision: " + llDetectedName(i) );
        }
    }

    collision_start(integer total_number)
    {
        integer i;
        for(i=0;i<total_number;i++)
        {
            llSay(0, "Collision Start: " + llDetectedName(i) );
        }
    }

    collision_end(integer total_number)
    {
        integer i;
        for(i=0;i<total_number;i++)
        {
            llSay(0, "Collision End: " + llDetectedName(i) );
        }
    }
}
```

Use your avatar to collide with the object. You will see which events are called. You will also notice that each of the events uses a for loop. This is because one event may report multiple avatars at once. It is somewhat rare that two avatars would be reported on exactly the same event. Because of this, many scripts just pass a zero into functions like **llDetectedName**. For example, the **collision_end** event could have been written as follows.

```
collision_end(integer total_number)
{
  llSay(0, "Collision End: " + llDetectedName(0) );
}
```

Unless a large number of avatars were colliding with the object simultaneously, the above code would work just fine.

It is also possible to detect collisions on a phantom object. A phantom object allows an avatar to pass through the object. Water is a very common example of a phantom object. To create your own water, simply use a water texture on a phantom object. You may have noticed that some water in Second Life causes a splash noise when an avatar jumps in. This can be done with collisions. However, you should call **llVolumeDetect(TRUE)** when dealing with a phantom object. Listing 7.3 shows a simple script that plays a splash sound for phantom water.

Listing 7.3: A Water Splash

```
default
{
    state_entry() {
        llVolumeDetect(TRUE);
    }

    collision_start( integer num_detected )
    {
        llTriggerSound("splash", 1);
    }

}
```

Any event that accepts a **num_detected** parameter can use the avatar and group detection functions, such as **llDetectedName**. You can also get the key of the avatar by using **llDetectedKey**. These functions will be covered in greater detail later in this section when object security is discussed.

Sensor Events

Sensors are another common type of event in Second Life. A sensor allows the object to know what avatars and other objects are around them. Sensors are notorious for their poor performance, so use them sparingly. Too many sensors in a Second Life region degrade overall performance.

Sensors are used for many different purposes in Second Life. Avatar radars can show which avatars are around. Notecard givers will sense avatars and hand out notecards. Sensor doors will open as an avatar approaches.

To use a sensor, the **llSensorRepeat** function should be called. The signature of the **llSensorRepeat** function is as follows.

```
llSensorRepeat( string name, key id, integer type, float range,
float arc, float rate );
```

The **name** specifies the name of the object or avatar to scan for. The **key** specifies the key of the object or avatar to scan for. The **type** parameter specifies the type of object to scan for. Specify **AGENT** to scan for avatars. Use **ACTIVE** to scan for moving objects or **PASSIVE** to scan for non-moving objects. One scanner can scan for multiple types, simply use the or (|) operator to scan. For example, to scan for both avatars and moving objects, use **AGENT|ACTIVE**. The **range** parameter specifies how far away to scan for. The **arc** parameter specifies how many degrees to scan over. This value is in radians, so specifying **PI** will scan all around. Finally, the **rate** parameter specifies how frequently to scan.

The following shows how to call **llSensorRepeat** to scan for avatars. It will scan from all directions up to 20 meters away. It will scan once a second.

```
llSensorRepeat("", "",AGENT, 20, PI, 1);
```

A notecard giver is a script that will hand out notecards to avatars that approach it. Notecard givers are a common use of scanners. Listing 7.4 shows a notecard giver.

Listing 7.4: Notecard Giver

```
string notecard = "Welcome Notecard";
integer freq = 1;
integer maxList = 100;
list given;


default
{
    state_entry()
    {
        llSensorRepeat("", "",AGENT, 20, PI, freq);
```

```
        llSetText("", <1.0, 1.0, 1.0>, 1.0);
    }

    sensor(integer num_detected)
    {
        integer i;
        key detected;

        for(i=0;i<num_detected;i++)
        {
            detected = llDetectedKey(i);

            if( llListFindList(given, [detected]) < 0 )
            {
                given += llDetectedKey(i);

                llGiveInventory(detected, notecard);
                if (llGetListLength(given) >= maxList)
                {
                    given = llDeleteSubList(given,0,10);
                }
            }
        }
    }
}
```

The sensor event is called at the interval specified by the frequency. In this case, the sensor event is called once a second. The sensor event begins by looping over all the avatars detected.

```
for(i=0;i<num_detected;i++)
{
        detected = llDetectedKey(i);
```

Once the **key** for the detected avatar is found, it is checked against the list of already found avatars. It is annoying for the notecard giver to keep handing out notecards to the same avatar. So the list tracks the last 10 avatars that it has given a card to.

```
        if( llListFindList(given, [detected]) < 0 )
        {
```

If the avatar has not had a card given to them, then add the avatar's key to the list.

```
            given += llDetectedKey(i);
```

Give an item to the detected user. The **llGiveInventory** function will give an item from the object's inventory. The object inventory is the same place that the script was created, which is the contents tab for the object. Simply drag an object to the content and it will be added to the object's inventory. You will now see the object, along with the script, in the content pane of the object properties.

```
llGiveInventory(detected, notecard);
```

If there are more items than the **maxList**, remove the oldest item.

```
if (llGetListLength(given) >= maxList)
{
        given = llDeleteSubList(given,0,maxList);
}
    }
}
```

The above script uses lists to track the avatars it has already passed out a notecard to. Lists are very useful for keeping data such as this. Lists will be covered in greater detail in Chapter 8.

Money Events

If a money event is present in a script, the user has the option to right-click the object and choose to pay that object. The **money** event has the following signature.

```
money(key giver, integer amount)
```

The giver parameter specifies the key of the avatar that gave money. The amount parameter specifies the amount that was given. Tip jars are a common example of scripts that use money events. A simple tip jar is shown in Listing 7.5.

Listing 7.5: Tip Jar

```
integer CHANNEL = 55;
integer total;

updateText()
{
    string str = llKey2Name(llGetOwner()) + "'s Tip Jar\n";
    if( total>0 )
        str+= (string)total + " donated so far.";
    else
        str+= "Empty";

    llSetText(str, <0,1,0>, 1);
}

default
```

```
{
    on_rez(integer s)
    {
        llResetScript();
    }

    state_entry()
    {
        updateText();
        llListen(CHANNEL, "", llGetOwner(), "");
    }

    money(key giver, integer amount) {
        llSay(0, "Thanks for the " + (string)amount + "L$, "
            + llKey2Name(giver));
        total+=amount;
        updateText();
    }

    touch_start(integer count)
    {
        if(llDetectedKey(0)==llGetOwner())
        {
            llDialog(llDetectedKey(0),
            "Clear total amount?", ["Yes","No"], CHANNEL);
        }
    }

    listen(integer channel, string name, key id, string message)
    {
        if( message=="Yes" && id==llGetOwner() )
        {
            total = 0;
            updateText();
        }
    }
}
```

The above tip jar will accept tips and keep a running total of how many times it has received. If the owner touches the tip jar, the owner will be asked whether they would like to reset the total on the tip jar.

The money event begins by thanking the avatar that gave the tip.

```
llSay(0, "Thanks for the " + (string)amount + "L$, " +
llKey2Name(giver));
```

Next the total is updated and the **updateText** function is called to update the total.

```
total+=amount;
updateText();
```

The **updateText** function, as seen above, is a simple function that uses **llSetText** to change the object's text. Changing an object's text was covered in Chapter 6.

When the user selects to pay an object, a small payment dialog is shown. This dialog lists four predefined payment amounts, and may allow the user to enter their own payment amount. This dialog is shown in Figure 7.1.

Figure 7.1: A Payment Dialog

The appearance and function of this dialog can be changed. This is done using the **llSetPayPrice** function call. The signature for **llSetPayPrice** is shown here.

```
llSetPayPrice(default, [price 1, price 2, price 3, price 4]);
```

The default is the default price. This is also where the user enters their own price. The other parameters specify the other four preset prices. To disable any of these, specify **PAY_HIDE**. For example, the following call to **llSetPayPrice** allows only 100 lindens to be entered.

```
llSetPayPrice(PAY_HIDE, [100, PAY_HIDE, PAY_HIDE, PAY_HIDE]);
```

Because **PAY_HIDE** was specified for the default price, the use is not allowed to enter their own price. Only the price of 100 is allowed.

It is also possible to have a script pay avatars. However, before a script can pay from the owner's money, permission must be obtained. This is covered in the next section.

Handling Permissions

It is also possible for a script to give money. However, giving money requires special permission. When a script that needs to take money from you is run, a special permission dialog is displayed. This dialog can be seen in Figure 7.2.

Figure 7.2: Money Dialog

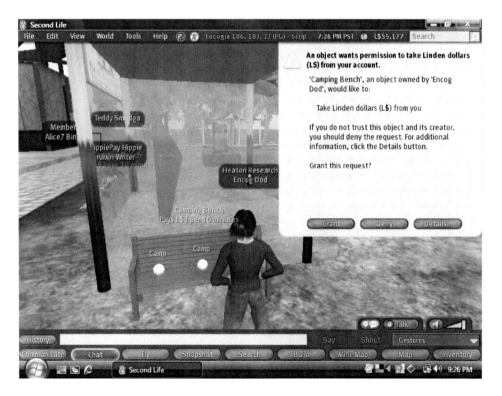

This will be used to make a simple guessing game. This game can be seen in Listing 7.6.

Listing 7.6: Guessing Game

```
integer answer;
integer INTERVAL = 10;
integer PRIZE = 1;

askQuestion()
{
    integer add1 = (integer)llFrand(11);
    integer add2 = (integer)llFrand(11);
    answer = add1+add2;
    llSay(0,"Would you like to win "+(string)PRIZE
            +" Linden Dollar(s)?");
    llSay(0,"Answer this question.  What is " + (string)add1 + "
            +" + (string)add2);
}

default
{
    state_entry()
    {
        llRequestPermissions(llGetOwner(), PERMISSION_DEBIT );
    }

    on_rez(integer s)
    {
        llResetScript();
    }

    run_time_permissions (integer perm)
    {
        if(perm & PERMISSION_DEBIT)
        {
            state ready;
        }
    }
}

state ready
{
    state_entry()
    {
        llSetTimerEvent(INTERVAL*60);
        llListen( 0, "", NULL_KEY, "" );
```

```
        askQuestion();
    }

    listen( integer channel, string name, key id, string message )
    {
        integer num = (integer)message;
        if( answer!=-1 && num>0 && (num==answer) )
        {

            llSay(0,"Congratulations " + name
                  + " you win the prize.");
            llSay(0,"Next question in " + (string)INTERVAL
                  + " minutes.");
            answer = -1;
            llGiveMoney(id,PRIZE);
        }
    }

    touch(integer detected)
    {
        if(llDetectedKey(0)==llGetOwner())
        {
            askQuestion();
        }
    }


    timer()
    {
        askQuestion();


    }
}
```

The above script begins by requesting permission to take money. The following line does this.

```
llRequestPermissions(llGetOwner(), PERMISSION_DEBIT );
```

The user's response will be relayed to the **run_time_permission** event. The signature of this event is as follows.

```
run_time_permissions (integer perm)
```

If the user gives permission to debit the account, the script then moves on to the **ready** state.

```
if(perm & PERMISSION_DEBIT)
{
```

```
        state ready;
}
```

To actually pay the user, the **llGiveMoney** function is used. The following line of code does this.

```
llGiveMoney(id,PRIZE);
```

The above script uses this line to give a user money for answering its simple question correctly.

The above script implements a simple function, named **askQuestion** that formulates a simple addition problem. Two random numbers are chosen. The user is then asked what the answer is.

```
integer add1 = (integer)llFrand(11);
integer add2 = (integer)llFrand(11);
answer = add1+add2;
```

The **llFrand** function creates a floating point number between 0 and one short of the number specified. This number is converted into an integer. The answer is then calculated. The script implements a listen event that then waits for the answer. If a correct answer is given, the avatar who answered is paid a small prize.

Implementing Basic Security

Some objects will only function when their owner is trying to use them. It is also possible to program an object to only function with group members. The following sections show how to implement basic security both for the owner and for groups.

Implementing Owner Security

Sometimes an object will only work with the owner of that object. This is particularly true of vehicles. The following script shows how to detect if someone, other than the owner, is trying to use the object. Listing 7.7 shows this.

Listing 7.7: Owner Security

```
default
{
    touch_start(integer total_number)
    {
        integer i;
        for(i=0;i<total_number;i++)
        {
            if( llDetectedKey(i)!=llGetOwner() )
            {
                llSay(0, llDetectedName(i)
                    + " you are not my owner.");
```

```
                    }
                    else
                    {
                        llSay(0, llDetectedName(i)
                            + " you are my owner.");
                    }
                }
            }
        }
```

When the above script is touched, the above script's **touch_start** event handler is called. The **touch_start** event handler is passed a value that indicates how many avatars are touching it at once. It is very rare that more than one avatar will be touching the object at once. However, if the object is likely to have more than one avatar touching at once, the script should make use of the **total_number** parameter.

This script makes use of the **total_number** parameter. A loop counts through all of the avatars that have touched the object. The **key** to each touching avatar is obtained with **llDetectedKey**. This **key** is compared against the owner of the object. If the owner and touching avatar are not the same, the avatar is informed that they are not welcome. This provides a quick method to determine whether an avatar is the owner or not.

Implementing Group Security

Sometimes an object will only work with the group of that object. The following script shows how to detect if someone, other than the group, is trying to use the object.

The group that an object is in can be set from the object properties window. Figure 7.3 shows an object with a group set.

Figure 7.3: Setting the Group of an Object

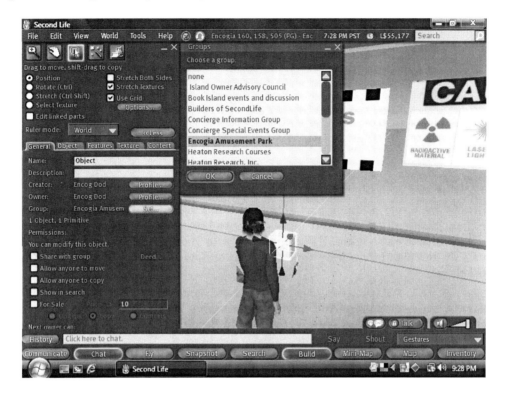

The following script checks to see whether the user that touched the object is in the same group as the object being touched. Listing 7.8 shows this.

Listing 7.8: Group Security

```
default
{
    touch_start(integer total_number)
    {
        integer i;
        for(i=0;i<total_number;i++)
        {
            if( llDetectedGroup(i)==FALSE )
            {
                llSay(0, llDetectedName(i)

                + " you must be in correct group.");
            }
            else
```

```
            {
                llSay(0, llDetectedName(i)
                  + " you are in my group.");
            }
        }
    }
}
```

To detect whether the touching avatar is in the same group as the object the **llDetectGroup** function is called. If the avatar is in the same group, then a value of **TRUE** is returned, otherwise **FALSE** is returned.

Summary

Events are a very common part of Second Life programming. Events are nothing more than functions with special names. These functions are called by Second Life when a specific event occurs. By adding events to your script, you can handle these events. Events are the primary way that your scripts are aware of what is going on around them.

Arrays are a common part of many programming languages. Arrays allow a list of items to be stored. Unfortunately, the Linden Scripting Language does not support arrays. Rather a special object type called a list is used. The list object type will be covered in the next chapter. The list object type allows the Linden Scripting Language to perform many of the same tasks that other languages perform with arrays. Additionally, lists are more flexible than arrays in many respects.

CHAPTER 8: LISTS

- Adding and Removing From a List
- Accessing a List
- Strided Lists
- Searching a List

Second Life does not support arrays. To keep a collection of variables a **list** must be used. Lists are much more advanced than the arrays provided by most other programming languages. Lists can hold any sort of variable, as an **integer** or **float**. Lists can also hold objects, such as a **vector** or **rotation**. The **list** object can even contain other lists.

A **list** is declared by using the **list** type. The following line of code declares an empty **list**.

```
list myList;
```

Additionally, lists can be declared with items already in the **list**. The following **list** contains four numbers.

```
list myList = [ 1, 2, 3, 4 ];
```

As stated previously, a **list** can contain more than one type of item. The following **list** is declared to hold two numbers and a **string**.

```
list myList = [ 1, 2, "Three" ];
```

Once the **list** has been declared it is ready for use.

Adding and Removing Items to Lists

Adding and removing data from lists is one of the most common **list** operations. In this section you will learn how to add and remove data from a **list**.

Adding Data to a List

Adding and removing items from a **list** is fairly easy. The addition operator (+) is used to combine two lists, for example, lists named **listA** and **listB**.

```
list listA = [1,2];
list listB = [3,4];
```

The addition operator can now be used to add these two lists together.

```
list listC = listA + listB;
```

The object **listC** now contains four numbers, the values 1,2,3 and 4. The two lists have been combined. This is the only way to add items to a **list**. The item must already be in another **list**. Fortunately, lists can be created on the fly. If you had a **string** named **str** that you wanted to add to a **list**, the following would do it.

```
string str = "Hello World";

list myList;
myList+= [ str ];
```

The above code creates a temporary **list** and adds it to the **list** named **myList**. The **+=** operator is a shorthand form of the following.

```
myList = myList + [str];
```

You can use either notation in your script. It is simply a matter of what you find the most readable.

Removing Data from Lists

Data can be removed from any location in the **list**. Additionally, multiple **list** items can be removed with a single function call. To remove items from a **list** use the **llDeleteSubList** function. The following lines of code demonstrate how to delete from a **list**.

```
list colors = ["Red", "Green", "Blue", "Yellow",
          "Black", "Orange"];
names = llDeleteSubList(names, 1, 2);
```

The above code would delete from position one to position two. This would result in the colors Green and Blue being deleted. It is important to note that lists begin at array element zero.

To delete all of the items in a **list**, assign the **list** to a new empty **list**. The following line of code would delete all items from **myList**.

```
myList = [];
```

After the above line was executed **myList** would be empty.

Retrieving Data from Lists

There are several ways to retrieve data from a **list**. The easiest is simply to use is **llDumpList2String**. The **llDumpList2String** function is only suitable for debugging purposes as it does not format the **list** in any way. To see how a variety of objects are displayed, consider Listing 8.1.

Listing 8.1: Dumping List Data

```
default
{

    touch_start(integer total_number)
    {
        list myList = [1, 2.0, "a string", llGetOwner()];
        llOwnerSay("<" + llDumpList2String(myList,"><") + ">");


    }
}
```

To execute the above script, touch the object that contains it. The above code would display the following line.

```
<1><2.000000><a string><c0c1c1ba-402e-4b31-a569-200f42a6335e>
```

If you execute the above line, your results will be somewhat different. The above key is unique to my avatar. The call to **llGetOwner** will return a different result depending on who the owner is.

The usual method for accessing the data is to call one of the **llList2** functions. These functions access a specific **list** item as a specific type. There are seven in all. They are summarized in Table 8.1.

Table 8.1: Accessing Data in a List

Function	Purpose
llList2Integer	Retrieve an integer from the list.
llList2Key	Retrieve a key from the list.
llList2List	Retrieve a list from the list.
llList2ListStrided	Retrieve a strided list from the list. Strided lists will be covered later in this chapter.
llList2Rot	Do not use, will return a zero rotation. It is better to use (rotation)llList2String(src, index).
llList2String	Retrieve a string from the list.
llList2Vector	Do not use, will return a zero vector. It is better to use (vector)llList ist2String(src, index).

The script shown in Listing 8.2 will display a **list** using **llList2String** and a loop.

Listing 8.2: Display a List

```
default
{
    touch_start(integer total_number)
    {
        list colors = ["Red", "Green", "Blue", "Yellow",
            "Black", "Orange"];
        integer i;
        for (i=0;i<llGetListLength(colors); ++i)
        {
            llOwnerSay( llList2String(colors,i) );
        }
    }
}
```

The above code will display all of the items in the colors **list**.

Lists and CSV

The comma-separated values (or CSV; also known as a comma-separated list or comma-separated variables) file format is a file type that stores tabular data. The format dates back to the early days of business computing. For this reason, CSV files are common on all computer platforms. Second Life implements its own special form of CSV. The Second Life form of CSV is not directly compatible with the generally accepted form of CSV. The Linden Scripting Language implements several functions that work with a Second Life's special form of CSV.

The Second Life form of CSV differs from the standard form of CSV in several important ways. First, the quote is not used around strings. A CSV string is simply comma separated. If you need to escape an element, enclose it in less-than (<) and greater-than (>) symbols. This allows a single element to contain a comma. The following is an example of a line of Second Life CSV values.

```
1, 2.000000, a string, <156.374557, 163.015213, 504.986145>
```

Notice the last element in the **list**? It is a **vector**. The enclosing < and > symbols prevent the commas inside the vector from causing the vector to be treated as three separate units. Because of the < and > symbols, the vector becomes one single element.

It is very convenient to use the Second Life CSV format. As you will recall from Chapter 6, strings can easily be communicated between objects. The CSV functions allow lists to easily be communicated between objects. Use the CSV functions to convert a **list** to a string. Then communicate the string. The object on the other end of the communication can then convert the CSV string back to a **list**.

Converting a List to CSV

To convert a **list** to CSV, use the **llList2CSV** function. Listing 8.3 shows how to do this.

Listing 8.3: Convert a List to CSV

```
default
{
    touch_start(integer total_number)
    {
        list myList = [1, 2.0, "a string", llGetPos()];
        string s = llList2CSV(myList);
        llOwnerSay(s);
    }
}
```

Calling **llList2CSV** will convert the above **list** into the following string.

```
1, 2.000000, a string, <156.374557, 163.015213, 504.986145>
```

Performing the reverse option is covered in the next section.

Converting CSV to a List

To convert a string back into a **list**, use the **llCSV2List** function. Listing 8.4 shows how this is done.

Listing 8.4: Convert CSV to a List

```
default
{
    touch_start(integer total_number)
    {
        string str = "1, 2.000000, a string,
            <156.374557, 163.015213, 504.986145>";
        list myList = llCSV2List(str);
        llSay(0,llDumpList2String(myList,","));
    }
}
```

The CSV string contained in the above script will be parsed to a **string**. The resulting **list** will then be displayed using **llDumpList2String**.

Parsing Strings

It is also possible to parse strings with delimiters other than just commas. The Linden Scripting Language provides two functions to parse general strings. They are summarized in Table 8.2.

Table 8.2: Accessing Data in a List

Function	Purpose
llParseString2List	Parse a list to a string using the specified delimiter.
llParseStringKeepNulls	Parse a list to a string using the specified delimiter. Keep any empty elements.

The above two functions work just like the CSV functions, except that you are allowed to specify the delimiter, or what separates the values.

List Statistics

Statistics can be gathered on a **list**. This provides for a quick way to take the sum, average, or another statistic on the numbers. To obtain statistics on a **list**, use the **llListStatistics** function. The signature for the **llListStatistics** function is shown here.

```
float llListStatistics( integer operation, list src )
```

The operation types are summarized in Table 8.3.

Table 8.3: Statistic Types

Statistic Type	Purpose
LIST_STAT_RANGE	Returns the range.
LIST_STAT_MIN	Retrieves the smallest number.
LIST_STAT_MAX	Retrieves the largest number.
LIST_STAT_MEAN	Retrieves the mean (average).
LIST_STAT_MEDIAN	Retrieves the median number.
LIST_STAT_STD_DEV	Calculates the standard deviation.
LIST_STAT_SUM	Calculates the sum.
LIST_STAT_SUM_SQUARES	Calculates the sum of the squares.
LIST_STAT_NUM_COUNT	Retrieves the number of float and integer elements.
LIST_STAT_GEOMETRIC_MEAN	Calculates the geometric mean.

Listing 8.5 shows an example of collecting statistics. This simple script calculates all of the statistics shown in the previous table, for a **list** containing the numbers one through ten.

Listing 8.5: Getting List Statistics

```
default
{
    touch_start(integer total_number)
    {
        list myList = [ 1, 2, 3, 4, 5, 6, 7, 8, 9, 10 ];

        llSay(0, "LIST_STAT_RANGE: " + (string)
            llListStatistics(LIST_STAT_RANGE, myList) );
        llSay(0, "LIST_STAT_MIN: " + (string)
            llListStatistics(LIST_STAT_MIN, myList) );
        llSay(0, "LIST_STAT_MAX: " + (string)
            llListStatistics(LIST_STAT_MAX, myList) );
        llSay(0, "LIST_STAT_MEAN: " + (string)
            llListStatistics(LIST_STAT_MEAN, myList) );
        llSay(0, "LIST_STAT_MEDIAN: " + (string)
            llListStatistics(LIST_STAT_MEDIAN, myList) );
        llSay(0, "LIST_STAT_STD_DEV: " + (string)
            llListStatistics(LIST_STAT_STD_DEV, myList) );
        llSay(0, "LIST_STAT_SUM: " + (string)
            llListStatistics(LIST_STAT_SUM, myList) );
        llSay(0, "LIST_STAT_SUM_SQUARES: " + (string)
            llListStatistics(LIST_STAT_SUM_SQUARES, myList) );
        llSay(0, "LIST_STAT_NUM_COUNT: " + (string)
            llListStatistics(LIST_STAT_NUM_COUNT, myList) );
        llSay(0, "LIST_STAT_GEOMETRIC_MEAN: " + (string)
            llListStatistics(LIST_STAT_GEOMETRIC_MEAN, myList) );
    }
}
```

When executed, this script produces the following output.

```
[11:28]  Object: LIST_STAT_RANGE: 9.000000
[11:28]  Object: LIST_STAT_MIN: 1.000000
[11:28]  Object: LIST_STAT_MAX: 10.000000
[11:28]  Object: LIST_STAT_MEAN: 5.500000
[11:28]  Object: LIST_STAT_MEDIAN: 5.500000
[11:28]  Object: LIST_STAT_STD_DEV: 3.027650
[11:28]  Object: LIST_STAT_SUM: 55.000000
[11:28]  Object: LIST_STAT_SUM_SQUARES: 385.000000
[11:28]  Object: LIST_STAT_NUM_COUNT: 10.000000
[11:28]  Object: LIST_STAT_GEOMETRIC_MEAN: 4.528728
```

Statistics can be a quick way to perform an operation over a **list** that would otherwise require looping across each **list** element.

Sorting, Searching and Striding Lists

Second Life does not support a two-dimensional array and lists are one-dimensional. Despite the fact that lists are one-dimensional, they support something called a stride. A stride simulates a two dimensional array with a one dimensional array. Consider an array that would store a **list** of products that will be sold in Second Life. You would like to store the following two values for each product:

- Product Name
- Product Price

A strided **list** could be used to store these items.

```
list products = [ "Jet Pack",25, "Blue Car", 100, "Black Hat",
    50 ];
```

Notice how each product contains two **list** items? There are really only three items in the **list**, not six. There are three groups of two. This **list** uses a stride of two. Using this stride allows the **list** to be thought of as a list of products.

Sorting Lists

Lists can be sorted using the **llListSort** function. The signature for the **llListSort** function is shown here.

```
list llListSort( list src, integer stride, integer ascending )
```

A **list** is provided that is to be sorted for the **src** parameter. The stride is specified in the stride parameter. If there is no stride, specify 1. Then a value of **TRUE** is specified for the ascending parameter if the sort is to be ascending.

Consider calling the **llListSort** function on the above **list** as follows.

```
products = llListSort( products, 2, TRUE);
```

The above function call would sort the **list** of products by the product name. The first element of a strided group is always what is sorted. Therefore it is important to choose the first element of a strided group carefully. In the case of the above **list**, the product name is the first element of each group. Therefore, the **list** is sorted by product name.

Randomizing Lists

In addition to sorting, lists can also be randomized. To randomize a list, use the **llListRandomize** function. The **llListRandomize** function has the following signature.

```
list llListRandomize( list src, integer stride );
```

The following call would randomize the **list** of products.

```
products = llListRandomize( products, 2 );
```

It is important to note that both the **llListSort** and **llListRandomize** functions return entirely new lists. This is why the results of both calls were assigned to the products **list**.

Searching Lists

It is also possible to search a **list**. This is done using the **llListFindList** function. Unfortunately, the **llListFindList** function does not support strides. If you would like to search a strided **list,** do it as a regular **list**. The signature for the **llListFindList** function is shown here.

```
integer llListFindList( list src, list test )
```

The first parameter, named **src**, is the **list** to search. The second parameter, named **test**, is what is being searched for. For example, to search **myList** for the name "Tom" the following function call would be used.

```
integer i = llListFindList( myList, ["Tom"] );
```

This would place the index of the first occurrence of the string "Tom" into the variable i. If "Tom" is not found, i will be set to -1. The search is case sensitive.

Summary

The Linden Scripting Language does not support arrays. To store lists of objects and variables the Linden Scripting Language, use lists. This chapter showed how to work with lists of objects and variables.

A **list** is one dimensional. Records cannot be stored in a **list**. To support something equivalent to a two-dimensional array, the Linden Scripting Language supports strided lists. A strided **list** a single **list** grouped together. For example, to store the name and price of an item into a strided **list**, use a stride of two. The elements in the **list** would be pairs, where each element pair makes up a single item.

So far this book has focused on the mechanics of the Linden Scripting Language. Other than communication, little interaction with the outside world has occurred. The remainder of the book will show how to interact with the objects that contain the scripts. The objects can be modified directly, or they can be moved. Movement can occur in two ways, physical or non-physical. The next chapter introduces non-physical movement.

CHAPTER 9: NON-PHYSICAL MOVEMENT

- Adding and Removing From a List
- Accessing a List
- Strided Lists
- Searching a List

In the previous chapters we created objects that interact with the world around them by communicating. There are many other ways that objects can interact. They can move in two ways. The first is physical movement. Physical movement occurs when objects follow the rules of physics. Objects move because forces act upon the objects.

The second way that objects can move is through the direct manipulation of their x, y and z coordinates. Every object has three numbers associated with it that specify that object's location. This chapter will show you how to move objects by manipulating their coordinates. However, before we begin, it is important to understand how Second Life represents coordinates.

Second Life Coordinates

The Second Life world is a large grid of regions. When you look at the map, you see regions. Figure 9.1 shows the Second Life map with several regions visible.

Figure 9.1: Gyeonu and Surrounding Regions

The area you are viewing in Figure 9.1 is called mainland. Mainland is a very large grid of regions that people can buy and sell individual plots of land. There are other regions near Gyenou. To the north and south are the regions of Chumong and Walcha Plane. To the east and west are Haemosu and Jiknyeo.

In addition to mainland, there are private islands. Private islands do not have neighboring regions unless the island owner buys addition islands. Whenever someone refers to "buying an island" in Second Life, they mean buying a private region, away from the mainland. The island of Encogia, where this book's examples reside, is a private island. Figure 9.2 shows the map near the island of Encogia. Notice there are no regions immediately adjacent to Encogia Island.

Figure 9.2: Encogia Island

Non-physical movement occurs entirely within a region. A region has its own x, y and z-coordinates. The x, y and z coordinates start over when a region's boundary is crossed. Inside of a region the x and y coordinates are flat on the ground. The z coordinate extends up and down. Figure 9.3 shows the x, y and z coordinates laid out on a box. The up and down arrow is the z coordinate. The x and y extend on the ground.

Figure 9.3: The Coordinate System

You can always see the current x, y and z coordinates at the top of the Second Life screen. Look at the top of Figure 9.3, at the same level as the menu bar. You will see the region name of Encogia, followed by three numbers. These three numbers are the x, y and z coordinates. If you fly up, the z-coordinate increases. If you fly down, the z coordinate decreases. Movement east and west affects the x coordinate. Similarly, movement north and south affects the y coordinate.

Every object in Second Life has an x, y and z coordinate. The Linden Scripting Language gives you functions to change the coordinates of an object. If you change the coordinate of an object, the object will move. However, changing the coordinates of any object will only move the object within a region. To move an object across a region boundary, physical movement must be used. Physical movement is covered in the next chapter.

Displaying an Object's Location and Rotation

The two most basic attributes of an object are its position and rotation. Both are expressed in terms of the three coordinates. To get the current position of an object call **llGetPos**. To get the current rotation of an object call **llGetRot**. Calling **llGetPos** will return a vector. A vector contains x, y and z components. The x and y coordinates range from 0,0 at the southwest corner of a region to 255,255 at the northeast corner of a region. The z coordinate starts at zero, below ground and goes up to 65,556 very high in the air. In all practicality you will not go that high into the air. Avatars cannot fly beyond 200 without a jet pack and you cannot build beyond about 1000.

Listing 9.1 shows a simple script that uses **llGetPos** to display the current position of the object that contains the script.

Listing 9.1: Display Current Position

```
default
{
    touch_start(integer total_number)
    {
        rotation rot = llGetRot();
        vector vrot = llRot2Euler(rot);
        llSay(0,"X-Rotation: " + (string)(vrot.x*RAD_TO_DEG) );
        llSay(0,"Y-Rotation: " + (string)(vrot.y*RAD_TO_DEG) );
        llSay(0,"Z-Rotation: " + (string)(vrot.z*RAD_TO_DEG) );
    }
}
```

As you can see from the above listing, the current position is stored into a **vector** variable named **pos**. The x, y and z components can be accessed directly. For example **pos.x** will access the **x** component of the position.

Rotations in Second Life are not stored in a vector object. Rather, they are stored in **rotation** objects. A **rotation** object has four components, **x**, **y**, **z** and **s**. These are called quaternions. A quaternion is a mathematical concept beyond the scope of this book. Most scripts do not directly deal with quaternions. Rather, quaternions are usually converted to regular **x**, **y** and **z** rotation. This is done using the **llEuler2Rot** and **llRot2Euler** functions. For example, to display the current **rotation** of any object a script such as Listing 9.2 would be used.

Listing 9.2: Display the Current Rotation

```
default
{
    touch_start(integer total_number)
    {
        rotation rot = llGetRot();
        vector vrot = llRot2Euler(rot);
        llSay(0,"X-Rotation: " + (string)(vrot.x*RAD_TO_DEG) );
        llSay(0,"Y-Rotation: " + (string)(vrot.y*RAD_TO_DEG) );
        llSay(0,"Z-Rotation: " + (string)(vrot.z*RAD_TO_DEG) );
    }
}
```

As you can see from the above code, the **rotation** is first obtained and placed in a variable named **rot**. The **llRot2Euler** function is then used to convert the **rotation** to a vector named **vrot**. The variable **vrot** now contains the **x**, **y** and **z** rotations in radian form. These values are now printed out. Multiplying by the **DEG_TO_RAD** constant will convert the radians to degrees.

Changing and Object's Location and Rotation

There are two functions named **llSetPos** and **llSetRot** that can be used to change the location of an object. Often, you will want to change the position of an object based on its previous position. For example, adding one to the z-coordinate will move the object up into the air slightly. Listing 9.3 shows a simple script that keeps increasing the x-coordinate.

Listing 9.3: Changing Object Location

```
default
{
    state_entry()
    {
        llSetTimerEvent(1);
    }

    timer()
    {
        vector pos = llGetPos();
        pos.x++;
        llSetPos(pos);
        llOwnerSay("I am at: " + (string)pos );
    }
}
```

The above script will move its object forward in the x direction. The script obtains the current position and then adds one to the x-coordinate. Eventually, the x coordinate will become too large and the object will be removed. When this happens, you will get a message similar to the following.

```
Second Life: Your object 'Object' has been returned to your in-
ventory lost and found folder from parcel 'Scripting Examples for
Second Life' at Encogia 257.747, 213.534 because it went off-
world.
```

It is also possible to change the object's rotation using **llSetRot**. Listing 9.4 shows a simple script that rotates an object.

Listing 9.4: Changing Object Rotation

```
default
{
    state_entry()
```

```
    {
        llSetTimerEvent(1);
    }

    timer()
    {
        rotation rot = llGetRot();
        vector vrot = llRot2Euler(rot);

        vrot+=<0,0,10*DEG_TO_RAD>;

        rot = llEuler2Rot(vrot);
        llSetRot(rot);
    }
}
```

The script begins by obtaining the current rotation as the variable **rot**. Next the current **rotation** is converted to a vector using **llRot2Euler**. The **rotation** is then moved by ten degrees on the z-axis. The number ten is converted to radians using the **DEG_TO_RAD** constant. Next, the **vector** is converted back into a **rotation** when is then set for the object using **llSetRot**.

The above script gives you absolute control over the rotation of an object. However, if you only want an object to endlessly rotate on one or more axes there is a much more efficient way to do it. The **llTargetOmega** allows you to preset a **rotation** on one or more axes. The object will continue to rotate without any need for a **timer** event. Listing 9.5 shows how to use **llTargetOmega**.

Listing 9.5: Rotation with llTargetOmega

```
default
{
    state_entry()
    {
        llTargetOmega(<0,0,1>,PI,1.0);
    }
}
```

The first parameter specifies which axis to rotate about. The second parameter is the spin rate. The third is the gain. The gain specifies the amount of force in the spin. For non-physical objects, this value is not used and is generally set to one.

A Touring Balloon

With the material covered this far in the book, a complex example can now be presented. A touring hot-air balloon will be created. This balloon will allow several passengers to sit in the balloon and take a tour of a region. The balloon can be seen in Figure 9.4.

Figure 9.4: A Touring Balloon

The balloon must be preprogrammed with a course to follow. This is done through a notecard. The notecard used for the balloon on the Encogia Island is shown in Listing 9.6.

Listing 9.6: Configuring the Balloon

```
<184.440,73.236,50>,Balloon has reached 50 meters. Beginning tour.
<244,123,50>,This is the bay of Encogia Beach. From here you can
see the ferris wheel.
<244,193,50>,The Heaton Research Tower is to the left. Heaton Re-
search is the sponsor of this island.
<240,242,50>, From here you can see the sky lift.  This ride al-
lows you to cross the bay.
<181,248,50>, Make sure you try the log ride.
<100,249,50>, Now flying over the back part of the island.  The is-
land owners and staff live here.  Ahead is Roman Yongho's house.
<13,169,50>, Flying over the back of the island.
<22,75,50>, Ahead is Encog Dod's home.  Encog built much of this
island.
<70,10,50>, Now returning to the amusement park.
<126,14,50>,To the left is the bumper car ride.  Balloon is head-
ing back.
<182.461,73.236,50>,Balloon has returned to base.
```

```
<184.440,773.236,21.652>,Balloon is landing.
```

Each line in the configuration card specifies one waypoint on the balloon's tour. There are two values, separated by a comma. The first is the vector of the waypoint. This is the x, y and z-coordinates of the waypoint. The second value specifies a **string** that the balloon will "say" upon arrival at that waypoint.

The source code for the script for the touring balloon is shown in Listing 9.7.

Listing 9.7: A Touring Balloon

```
float SPEED = 1;
vector target;
list waypoints;
integer currentWaypoint;
string message;

// for loading notecard
string notecardName = "Configure Balloon";
key notecardQuery;
integer notecardIndex;

integer nextWayPoint()
{
    if( currentWaypoint>= llGetListLength(waypoints) )
    {
        llSay(0,"Ride over");
        return TRUE;
    }
    else
    {
        target = llList2Vector(waypoints,currentWaypoint);
        message = llList2String(waypoints,currentWaypoint+1);
        currentWaypoint+=2;
        return FALSE;
    }
}


default
{
    state_entry()
    {
        llSay(0,"Balloon loading waypoints...");
        notecardIndex = 0;
        notecardQuery = llGetNotecardLine(notecardName,
            notecardIndex++);
    }
```

```
dataserver(key query_id, string data)
{
    if ( notecardQuery == query_id)
    {
        // this is a line of our notecard
        if (data == EOF)
        {
            llSay(0,"Data loaded, balloon ready...");
            state waiting;

        } else
        {

            list temp = llCSV2List(data);

            vector vec = (vector)llList2String(temp,0);
            string str = llList2String(temp,1);
            waypoints+=[vec,str];
            notecardQuery = llGetNotecardLine(notecardName,
                    notecardIndex++);
        }
    }
}
}

state running
{
    state_entry()
    {
        currentWaypoint = 0;
        nextWayPoint();
        llSetTimerEvent(0.1);
    }

    timer()
    {
        vector pos = llGetPos();
        integer match = 0;

        if( llFabs(pos.x - target.x) < SPEED )
        {
            pos.x = target.x;
            match++;
        }
        else
```

```
        {
            if( pos.x > target.x )
                pos.x-=SPEED;
            else
                pos.x+=SPEED;
        }

        if( llFabs(pos.y - target.y) < SPEED )
        {
            pos.y = target.y;
            match++;
        }
        else
        {
            if( pos.y > target.y )
                pos.y-=SPEED;
            else
                pos.y+=SPEED;
        }

        if( llFabs(pos.z - target.z) < SPEED )
        {
            pos.z = target.z;
            match++;
        }
        else
        {
            if( pos.z > target.z )
                pos.z-=SPEED;
            else
                pos.z+=SPEED;
        }

        llSetPos(pos);

        if( match==3 )
        {
            string hold = message;
            if( nextWayPoint() )
                state waiting;
            llSay(0,hold);
        }
    }
}

state waiting
```

```
{
    state_entry()
    {
        llSay(0,"Balloon is waiting.");
    }

    link_message(integer sender_num, integer num, string str, key
id)
    {
        if( str=="go" )
        {
            state countdown;
        }
    }
}

state countdown
{
    state_entry()
    {
        llSetTimerEvent(20);
        llSay(0,"Welcome to the balloon ride.  Balloon will launch
in 20 seconds.  Please take your seats!");
    }

    timer()
    {
        state running;
    }
}
```

The touring balloon is made up of four states. These states are listed here.

- default
- waiting
- countdown
- running

The **default** state does nothing more than load the configuration notecard. Once the notecard has been loaded, the **waiting** state is entered. The **waiting** state continues until someone sits in the balloon. Once the balloon enters the waiting state, it will wait for 20 seconds. This allows other people to board the balloon. When the 20 seconds is up the balloon enters the running state. In the **running** state, the balloon will begin following its waypoints until complete. Once the balloon has completed its course it enters the waiting state again.

Script Variables and Functions

There are several variables that are defined for the script to run.

```
float SPEED = 1;
vector target;
list waypoints;
integer currentWaypoint;
string message;
```

The **SPEED** variable can be set to however fast the balloon should travel. The higher the number, the faster the balloon. The target variable holds the current destination. The waypoints list holds the waypoints. The **currentWaypoint** holds the index of the current waypoint. The message variable holds the current message for the waypoint.

The waypoints list holds pairs of items. Each waypoint is made up of a vector location and a message to display. Because of this, the **currentWaypoint** index is increased by two each time a waypoint is reached.

There are also several variables used to read the notecard.

```
// for loading notecard
string notecardName = "Configure Balloon";
key notecardQuery;
integer notecardIndex;
```

The **notecardName** variable holds the name of the configuration notecard. The **notecardQuery** variable holds the key to the query of the notecard while it is being read. Finally, the **notecardIndex** variable holds the current line of the notecard.

A global function is also defined to move to the next waypoint. This function is called **nextWayPoint**.

```
integer nextWayPoint()
{
```

If the **currentWaypoint** variable has reached the end of the waypoints list, the ride is over. The value **TRUE** is returned to signify that.

```
    if( currentWaypoint>= llGetListLength(waypoints) )
    {
        llSay(0,"Ride over");
        return TRUE;
    }
```

If we have not reached the end, read the pair for the **currentWaypoint** index. The first value is the **target vector**. The second value is the message to display.

```
else
{
    target = llList2Vector(waypoints,currentWaypoint);
    message = llList2String(waypoints,currentWaypoint+1);
```

Increase the current waypoint by two to move past the pair. Return **FALSE** to signal that we have not reached the end.

```
    currentWaypoint+=2;
    return FALSE;
}
}
```

The **nextWaypoint** function is used at several locations within the balloon script.

Default State

All scripts begin in the **default** state. The **default** state for the balloon ride is responsible for loading the configuration notecard. Once the notecard has been read, the script will enter the **waiting** state.

```
default
{
```

When the state is first entered, the balloon announces that it is loading the waypoints. The notecard index is reset to zero and the notecard is queried by reading the first line.

```
    state_entry()
    {
        llSay(0,"Balloon loading waypoints...");
        notecardIndex = 0;
        notecardQuery = llGetNotecardLine(notecardName,
            notecardIndex++);
    }
```

When a notecard line is queried, the response is not instant. However, the **dataserver** event will soon be called.

```
    dataserver(key query_id, string data)
    {
```

First, check to see whether the **query_id** matches the query that we requested. It is highly unlikely that data from any other query would enter this event; however, it is a good idea to perform this check.

```
                if ( notecardQuery == query_id)
                {
```

If this is our query, check to see whether the end has been reached. If an end-of-file (**EOF**) has been reached, announce that the balloon is ready and enter the **ready** state.

```
        // this is a line of our notecard
        if (data == EOF)
        {
            llSay(0,"Data loaded, balloon ready...");
            state waiting;

        } else
        {
```

If valid data has been found, parse the list. Each configuration item has two values separated by a comma. This is a valid Second Life CSV line therefore **llCSV2List** can be used to parse the line to a list.

```
        list temp = llCSV2List(data);
```

Obtain the **vector** and message from the **list**.

```
        vector vec = (vector)llList2String(temp,0);
        string str = llList2String(temp,1);
```

Add this pair of items to the waypoints **list**.

```
        waypoints+=[vec,str];
```

Query for the next line. This will cause the **dataserver** event to be called again with either the next line of an **EOF** value.

```
        notecardQuery = llGetNotecardLine(notecardName,
          notecardIndex++);
        }
      }
    }
}
```

After all of the configuration data has been loaded, the **default** state will end and the waiting state will begin.

Waiting State

The balloon is triggered into action when an avatar sits on it. While the balloon is waiting for an avatar to sit, it is in the waiting state.

```
state waiting
{
```

The **waiting** state begins by announcing that the balloon is waiting.

```
state_entry()
{
    llSay(0,"Balloon is waiting.");
}
```

When the user sits on one of the provided seats in the balloon, a **link_message** is sent. The script for each of the seats will be shown later in this chapter. However, it is a very simple script. The seat scripts send the a "go" message to the balloon when someone sits.

```
link_message(integer sender_num, integer num, string str, key id)
{
```

If it is a "go" message then enter the countdown state.

```
    if( str=="go" )
    {
        state countdown;
    }
}
}
```

The balloon will spend most of its life in the **waiting** state.

Countdown State

After the first passenger is seated in the balloon, the balloon will begin a countdown. This 20 second countdown allows other passengers to sit before the balloon departs. Providing this countdown is the job of the **countdown** state.

```
state countdown
{
```

When the **countdown** state begins a timer is set for 20 seconds. All of the timers seen so far have occurred at regular intervals. Timers can also be useful for a countdown to a single event. The timer will only reach one 20 second interval, and then the state will change. Because the state changes, the **countdown** state never gets a chance to reach the second 20 second interval.

```
state_entry()
{
    llSetTimerEvent(20);
    llSay(0,"Welcome to the balloon ride.  Balloon will launch
in 20 seconds.  Please take your seats!");
}
```

When the 20 second interval is reached, the **timer** event simply moves on to the **running** state.

```
timer()
{
    state running;
}
}
```

The **running** state is where the balloon navigates the waypoint list. The **running** state is discussed in the next section.

Running State

The **running** state is where the balloon performs all of its movements. The balloon makes use of non-physical movement. The **llSetPos** function is used to move the balloon around the region.

```
state running
{
```

When the **running** state first starts, the **currentWaypoint** is reset to zero. This ensures that the balloon begins at the beginning of the course. The **nextWayPoint** function is called to set the appropriate variables for travel to the first waypoint. Finally, a timer is set to occur ten times a second. This timer is used to move the balloon.

```
state_entry()
{
    currentWaypoint = 0;
    nextWayPoint();
    llSetTimerEvent(0.1);
}
```

All of the work of moving the balloon around the region is performed inside of the **timer** event. The **timer** event is relatively simple. The **timer** looks at the current position, then it looks at the target position. The x, y an z coordinates are adjusted to cause the current position to slowly move towards the **target** position.

```
timer()
{
```

First the current position is obtained. A local variable, named **match** is used to track how many of the three dimensions have reached the target waypoint. When all three match, it is time to move on to the next waypoint.

```
vector pos = llGetPos();
integer match = 0;
```

First check to see whether the x-coordinate has reached the target. If the x-coordinate has reached this, set the x-coordinate to exactly match the target x-coordinate.

```
if( llFabs(pos.x - target.x) < SPEED )
{
    pos.x = target.x;
    match++;
}
```

If the x-coordinate does need to be adjusted, check to see whether the x-coordinate is too large or too small. Increase or decrease the current x-coordinate as appropriate to cause it to become closer to the target x-coordinate.

```
else
{
    if( pos.x > target.x )
        pos.x-=SPEED;
    else
        pos.x+=SPEED;
}
```

Next, check to see whether the y-coordinate has reached the target. If the y-coordinate has reached this, set the y-coordinate to exactly match the target y-coordinate.

```
if( llFabs(pos.y - target.y) < SPEED )
{
    pos.y = target.y;
    match++;
}
```

If the y-coordinate needs to be adjusted, check to see whether the y-coordinate is too large or two small. Increase or decrease the current y-coordinate as appropriate to cause it to become closer to the target y-coordinate.

```
else
{
    if( pos.y > target.y )
        pos.y-=SPEED;
    else
        pos.y+=SPEED;
}
```

Next, check to see whether the z-coordinate has reached the target. If the z-coordinate has reached this, set the z-coordinate to exactly match the target z-coordinate.

```
if( llFabs(pos.z - target.z) < SPEED )
{
    pos.z = target.z;
    match++;
}
```

If the z-coordinate needs to be adjusted, check to see whether the z-coordinate is too large or two small. Increase or decrease the current z-coordinate as appropriate to make it closer to the target z-coordinate.

```
else
{
    if( pos.z > target.z )
        pos.z-=SPEED;
    else
        pos.z+=SPEED;
}
```

Finally, the **pos** variable will contain the new desired position. Call **llSetPos** to move to the new adjusted position.

```
llSetPos(pos);
```

Finally, check to see whether all three coordinates now match the target **vector**.

```
if( match==3 )
{
    string hold = message;
    if( nextWayPoint() )
        state waiting;
    llSay(0,hold);
}
    }
}
```

If all three coordinates match, move to the next waypoint. If the last waypoint has been reached, enter the waiting state. The current message is moved to the hold variable, so that it is not lost when we move to the next waypoint. Finally, the waypoint message is said.

Seat Scripts

The balloon contains several seats for passengers to sit on. It is convention in Second Life to represent sit-down areas as small balls that the user selects to sit down on. Generally pink balls are for females, blue for males, and yellow for gender neutral seating. Why does gender matter sometimes? For example, some dance poses that use balls for the avatars to sit on have specific parts to be played out by male vs female avatars.

The same seating script is placed inside of each of the seated balls. This script is shown in Listing 9.8.

Listing 9.8: Balloon Seat Script

```
default
{
    state_entry()
    {
        llSitTarget(<-0.1,-0.25,0.25>, ZERO_ROTATION );
        llSetText("Sit Here",<255,0,0>,1.0);
        llSetSitText("Sit Here");
    }

    changed(integer change)
    {
        key a = llAvatarOnSitTarget();
        if(a==NULL_KEY )
        {
            vector vec = <0.25,0.25,0.25>;
            llSetScale(vec);
            llSetText("Sit Here",<255,0,0>,1.0);
        }
        else
        {
            vector vec = <0.010,0.010,0.010>;
            llSetScale(vec);
            llSetText("",<255,0,0>,1.0);
            llMessageLinked(LINK_ROOT,0,"go",NULL_KEY);
```

The balloon seating script begins by setting the sit target. The avatar is to sit straight up and down so a **ZERO_ROTATION** works well. The appropriate text is also displayed just above the sit ball. Additionally, the sit text is replaced by "Sit Here". This changes the text on the popup menu when the user right-clicks the sit ball.

```
default
{
    state_entry()
    {
        llSitTarget(<-0.1,-0.25,0.25>, ZERO_ROTATION );
        llSetText("Sit Here",<255,0,0>,1.0);
        llSetSitText("Sit Here");
    }
```

When an avatar either sits down or stands up, the **changed** event is called.

```
changed(integer change)
{
```

Determine the avatar that has sat on the sit ball. This is done by calling the **llAvatarOnSitTarget** function.

```
key a = llAvatarOnSitTarget();
```

If a **NULL_KEY** is returned, the avatar has stood up.

```
if(a==NULL_KEY )
```

Restore the ball to its regular size and return the object text.

```
vector vec = <0.25,0.25,0.25>;
llSetScale(vec);
llSetText("Sit Here",<255,0,0>,1.0);
```

If an avatar is just sitting down, the sit ball should be shrunk to a very small size. This gets it out of the way while the avatar is sitting there. Additionally, the "Sit Here" text is hidden. Finally, the "go" message is sent to all linked objects with the **llMessageLinked** function call.

```
vector vec = <0.010,0.010,0.010>;
llSetScale(vec);
llSetText("",<255,0,0>,1.0);
llMessageLinked(LINK_ROOT,0,"go",NULL_KEY);
```

This balloon script can be very useful for giving tours of a region. These balloons are often used by visitors to Encogia island.

Summary

All objects in Second Life move around on regions. Inside of these regions are x, y and z-coordinates. The x and y coordinates express movement on the surface plane. The z-coordinate expresses movement up and down in altitude.

Second Life allows objects to move in two different ways. Objects can move physically, by having forces applied to them. Objects can also move non-physically by directly manipulating their x, y and z-coordinates. The rotation and position of an object can be set to achieve this movement.

Second Life positions are stored in the **vector** data type. Second Life rotations are stored in the rotation data type. A vector contains the x, y and z-coordinates of a position. A **rotation** is expressed as a 4-part number, called a quaternion. Few scripts use quaternions directly. Most scripts convert these quaternions into radians of rotation about the x, y and z-coordinates. The Linden Scripting Language provides several functions to perform these transformations.

It is also possible to move objects using physics. Physical movement requires a force to be applied to an object. Physics allows advanced vehicles, and other physical devices, to be created. Physical movement will be covered in the next section.

CHAPTER 10: PHYSICAL MOVEMENT AND VEHICLES

- Applying Force to an Avatar
- Understanding Force and Impulse
- Using Rotational and Linear Force
- Creating Vehicles

Second Life objects can also be moved physically. When an object is moved physically, it obeys the laws of physics. This means that to move the object, force must be applied to it. There are two ways to achieve physical movement:

- Direct Force Application
- Vehicle Motors

The simplest means of moving an object is to directly apply force to it. Functions are provided that apply either a constant or impulse force to an object. Additionally, this force can be applied to another object or avatar. We will first examine how to apply force to an avatar.

Applying Force to an Avatar

An object can detect collisions from other avatars and objects. Chapter 7, "Events" showed how to do this. By responding to these collisions with a small push upward, a simple trampoline can be constructed. Figure 10.1 shows a trampoline in Second Life.

Figure 10.1: A Trampoline

The script used to create this trampoline is shown in Listing 10.1.

Listing 10.1: Trampoline Script

```
default
{
    state_entry()
    {
        llPreloadSound("boing");
    }

    collision_start( integer num_detected )
    {
        integer i;
        for(i = 0;  i<num_detected;  i++ )
        {
            key k = llDetectedKey(i);
            if( k !=NULL_KEY )
            {
                llTriggerSound("boing",1);
                llPushObject(k, <0,0,25>, ZERO_VECTOR, FALSE);
```

```
            }
        }
    }
}
```

This script is contained entirely inside of the **default** state.

```
default
{
```

When the state is first entered, a sound is preloaded. This is a simple cartoon "boing" sound that will be played when someone makes contact with the trampoline.

```
    state_entry()
    {
        llPreloadSound("boing");
    }
```

Nearly all of the script functionality is contained inside of the **collision_start** event handler.

```
    collision_start( integer num_detected )
    {
```

There could be many avatars on the trampoline at once. Because of this, it is important to use the **num_detected** parameter to make sure that each avatar is properly "bounced". The **num_detected** parameter gives the number of avatars that have collided with this event.

```
        integer i;
        for(i = 0; i<num_detected; i++ )
        {
```

A **key** is obtained for each item that has collided with the trampoline.

```
            key k = llDetectedKey(i);
```

Make sure that this is a valid **key**.

```
            if( k !=NULL_KEY )
            {
```

It is now time to "bounce" an object. Play the "boing" sound and apply an upward push to the object. This is done using the **llPushObject**.

```
                llTriggerSound("boing",1);
                llPushObject(k, <0,0,25>, ZERO_VECTOR, FALSE);
            }
        }
    }
}
```

The **llPushObject** is used to apply a single force to an object. The signature for this function is shown here.

```
llPushObject(key id, vector impulse, vector angular_impulse, inte-
ger local)
```

The **id** variable specifies the object, or avatar, that is to be pushed. The **impulse vector** specifies how much force should be applied to the x, y and z-coordinates. The **angular_impulse** variable specifies how much angular force to apply to the x, y and z angles. Basically **angular_impulse** spins the object, whereas impulse changes the location of the object. Finally **local**, which should be **TRUE** or **FALSE**, specifies whether the push is relative to the object's rotation.

Applying Force to the Current Object

First of all, before force can be applied to an object, it must be marked as a "physical object". If force is applied to a non-physical object, there will be no effect. There are two ways to mark an object as physical. The first is to use the prim properties. Figure 10.2 shows an object being marked as physical using the prim properties.

Figure 10.2: Marking an Object as Physical

An object can also be marked as physical or non-physical programatically. This is very common for vehicles. A Second Life car will typically mark itself as physical when someone first sits down at the car and is ready to drive. Once the avatar has left the car, the car will mark itself as non-physical. This prevents the car from moving when other avatars bump into it. Marking the car non-physical sets the "parking brake".

To set the current object to physical, the following command is used.

```
llSetStatus(STATUS_PHYSICS, TRUE);
```

Similarly to set an object as non-physical, the following command is used.

```
llSetStatus(STATUS_PHYSICS, FALSE);
```

Once the current object is marked as physical, there are three ways to apply force to it.

- set a constant direct force
- apply an impulse
- use a vehicle motor

Using a vehicle motor will be explained in the next section. Usually, an impulse force will be applied. This force is applied once per function call and sets the object in motion at a speed dependent on how much force was applied. To apply an impulse force, use the **llApplyImpulse** function. The **llApplyImpulse** function has the following signature.

```
llApplyImpulse(vector force, integer local)
```

The first parameter specifies the amount of force to be applied to the current object. This **vector** specifies the amount of force to be applied to the x, y and z-coordinates. If the local parameter is **TRUE**, then the force is applied based on the object's rotation.

You may be wondering what values to specify for the force. Just as in real physics, the amount of movement a force will achieve is dependent on the mass of the object getting moved. For example, to move an object up at an acceleration of 10 meters per second, the following function call should be used.

```
llApplyImpulse( llGetMass() * <0,0,10>, FALSE );
```

Multiply the desired velocity, measured in meters per second, by the mass of the object. The above call will only apply a once-time impulse. Gravity will quickly overcome this force and the object will fall back to the ground. To apply a constant force, use the **llSetForce** function call.

```
llSetForce(<0,0,9.8*llGetMass()>,FALSE);
```

The above function call would set a constant force equal to 9.8 meters per second upward. This exactly counters the force of gravity, which has an acceleration of -9.8 meters per second. Another useful function call is to stop an object already in motion. This can be done with the following line of code.

```
llApplyImpulse(-llGetMass()*llGetVel(),FALSE);
```

This line of code obtains the object's current velocity and applies the exact force necessary to stop the object.

Rotational force can also be applied to objects. This will cause the object to spin. The **llApplyRotationalImpulse** function call is used to do this. The **llApplyRotationalImpulse** has the following signature.

```
llApplyRotationalImpulse(vector force, integer local);
```

The force vector specifies how much rotational force to apply in x, y and z-coordinates. If the local parameter is true, the rotation is relative to the object's current rotation.

Second Life Vehicles

The example car is a bright-red two seater convertible. The car is not a true convertible because it does not convert. It is always in top-down mode. Because it never rains in Second Life, this is not a problem! The little red sports car is shown in Figure 10.3.

Figure 10.3: A Car in Second Life

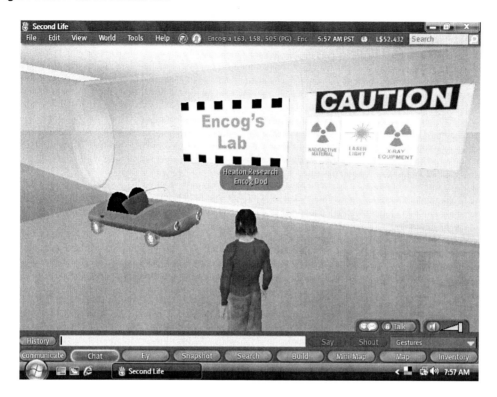

The next few sections will explain different aspects of the car, and how it was constructed and scripted.

Vehicle Materials

All prims in Second Life have a material. The following materials are supported in Second Life: stone, metal, glass, wood, flesh, plastic and rubber. Materials affect the mass and friction of the vehicle. The majority of prims in Second Life are made of wood. This is because wood is the default material. Material type is specified in the object window. Figure 10.4 shows the material type being set.

Figure 10.4: Setting the Material Type

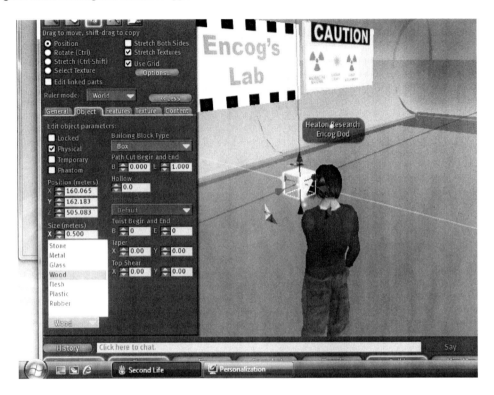

Material types are very important for vehicles in Second Life. The material type for the tires of the car is of particular importance. Which of the above material types should be chosen for the tires? Rubber may seem the logical choice. Rubber would create too much friction. Remember, that in the simplistic physics of Second Life, the tires do not really turn. They appear to turn, due to a trick used later in this example. But they are not really turning. Imagine a parked car being pushed along the ground. If the parking brake is on, that car will not move as efficiently. The rubber would burn and the car would merely bump along. This is what happens when the tires are made of rubber in Second Life. The car barely moves.

The material of choice is surprising. It is the material with the least friction - glass. Any part of the vehicle that comes into contact with the ground should be made of glass. Durability is not an issue with a prim! Glass wheels are the norm in Second Life. Don't think of the materials as the actual materials. Rather, think of the material types as specifying the amount of friction the prim will cause.

The Root Prim

The car, like any other object in Second Life, consists of several primitives. However, not all primitives are equal. The most important primitive, or prim, is the root prim. When an object is selected, the root prim is outlined in yellow. The root prim is a very important concept for vehicles.

The root prim is the last prim selected when the vehicle was linked together. Therefore, it is very easy to accidentally change the root prim when new prims are being added to the object. For example, consider adding a bumper sticker to the car. Consider if the car was selected, the bumper sticker shift-selected and a link created. The bumper sticker would now be a part of the car object. However, the bumper sticker would now be the root prim! The bumper sticker was the last prim selected, so it is now the root prim. This would prevent the car from functioning properly. This is because the car is designed for the driver's seat to be the root prim.

The correct way to add the bumper sticker to the car would be to do this procedure in reverse. First, select the bumper sticker. Then shift-select the car and create the link. Now the car is the last object selected and the root prim will not change.

The root primitive is critical to a vehicle because the root prim is where the main vehicle script resides. Think of the root prim as the motor for the vehicle. It is the root prim that is moving, everything else is only attached to the root prim. It is also convenient if the driver sits on the root prim. This is why most vehicles in Second Life always make the root prim the driver's seat.

It also makes vehicle creation considerably easier if the root prim is at zero rotation in all three directions. At the very least, the root prim should only be rotated in 90-degree intervals in the three dimensions.

The root prim must be made a physical object for the vehicle to operate. Normally, this is done in code using a call to **llSetStatus**. However, being physical imposes an important limitation on vehicles. Physical objects in Second Life can contain no more than 31 prims. Because of this, no vehicle can contain more than 31 prims. If prim number 32 is added, the vehicle will stop.

The root prim is where the main car script resides. The car script can be seen in Listing 10.2.

Listing 10.2: Main Car Script for the Root Prim (Car.lsl)

```
float forward_power = 15; //Power used to go forward (1 to 30)
float reverse_power = -15; //Power ued to go reverse (-1 to -30)
float turning_ratio = 2.0; //How sharply the vehicle turns. Less is
```

```
more sharply. (.1 to 10)
string sit_message = "Ride"; //Sit message
string not_owner_message = "You are not the owner of this vehicle
..."; //Not owner message

default
{
    state_entry()
    {
        llSetSitText(sit_message);
        // forward-back,left-right,updown
        llSitTarget(<0.2,0,0.45>, ZERO_ROTATION );

        llSetCameraEyeOffset(<-8, 0.0, 5.0>);
        llSetCameraAtOffset(<1.0, 0.0, 2.0>);

        llPreloadSound("car_start");
        llPreloadSound("car_run");

        //car
        llSetVehicleType(VEHICLE_TYPE_CAR);
        llSetVehicleFloatParam(
VEHICLE_ANGULAR_DEFLECTION_EFFICIENCY, 0.2);
        llSetVehicleFloatParam(
VEHICLE_LINEAR_DEFLECTION_EFFICIENCY, 0.80);
        llSetVehicleFloatParam(
VEHICLE_ANGULAR_DEFLECTION_TIMESCALE, 0.10);
        llSetVehicleFloatParam(
VEHICLE_LINEAR_DEFLECTION_TIMESCALE, 0.10);
        llSetVehicleFloatParam(
VEHICLE_LINEAR_MOTOR_TIMESCALE, 1.0);
        llSetVehicleFloatParam(
VEHICLE_LINEAR_MOTOR_DECAY_TIMESCALE, 0.2);
        llSetVehicleFloatParam(
VEHICLE_ANGULAR_MOTOR_TIMESCALE, 0.1);
        llSetVehicleFloatParam(
VEHICLE_ANGULAR_MOTOR_DECAY_TIMESCALE, 0.5);
        llSetVehicleVectorParam(
VEHICLE_LINEAR_FRICTION_TIMESCALE, <1000.0, 2.0, 1000.0>);
        llSetVehicleVectorParam(
VEHICLE_ANGULAR_FRICTION_TIMESCALE, <10.0, 10.0, 1000.0>);
        llSetVehicleFloatParam(
VEHICLE_VERTICAL_ATTRACTION_EFFICIENCY, 0.50);
        llSetVehicleFloatParam(
VEHICLE_VERTICAL_ATTRACTION_TIMESCALE, 0.50);
    }
```

```
changed(integer change)
{


    if (change & CHANGED_LINK)
    {

        key agent = llAvatarOnSitTarget();
        if (agent)
        {
            if (agent != llGetOwner())
            {
                llSay(0, not_owner_message);
                llUnSit(agent);
                llPushObject(agent, <0,0,50>,
                    ZERO_VECTOR, FALSE);
            }
            else
            {
                llTriggerSound("car_start",1);


                llMessageLinked(LINK_ALL_CHILDREN , 0,
                    "WHEEL_DRIVING", NULL_KEY);
                llSleep(.4);
                llSetStatus(STATUS_PHYSICS, TRUE);
                llSleep(.1);
                llRequestPermissions(agent,
PERMISSION_TRIGGER_ANIMATION | PERMISSION_TAKE_CONTROLS);

                llLoopSound("car_run",1);
            }
        }
        else
        {
            llStopSound();

            llSetStatus(STATUS_PHYSICS, FALSE);
            llSleep(.4);
            llReleaseControls();
            llTargetOmega(<0,0,0>,PI,0);

            llResetScript();
        }
    }
```

```
    }

    run_time_permissions(integer perm)
    {
        if (perm)
        {
            llTakeControls(CONTROL_FWD | CONTROL_BACK |
CONTROL_DOWN | CONTROL_UP | CONTROL_RIGHT |
CONTROL_LEFT | CONTROL_ROT_RIGHT | CONTROL_ROT_LEFT, TRUE, FALSE);
        }
    }

    control(key id, integer level, integer edge)
    {
        integer reverse=1;
        vector angular_motor;

        //get current speed
        vector vel = llGetVel();
        float speed = llVecMag(vel);

        //car controls
        if(level & CONTROL_FWD)
        {
            llSetVehicleVectorParam(
VEHICLE_LINEAR_MOTOR_DIRECTION, <forward_power,0,0>);
            reverse=1;
        }
        if(level & CONTROL_BACK)
        {
            llSetVehicleVectorParam(
VEHICLE_LINEAR_MOTOR_DIRECTION, <reverse_power,0,0>);
            reverse = -1;
        }

        if(level & (CONTROL_RIGHT|CONTROL_ROT_RIGHT))
        {
            angular_motor.z -= speed / turning_ratio * reverse;
        }

        if(level & (CONTROL_LEFT|CONTROL_ROT_LEFT))
        {
            angular_motor.z += speed / turning_ratio * reverse;
        }
```

```
          llSetVehicleVectorParam(
VEHICLE_ANGULAR_MOTOR_DIRECTION, angular_motor);


    }



}
```

The following sections explain the various parts of the car script.

Obtaining Permission

The car will be driven in a similar way to how an avatar walks. Cursor keys will turn and move it forward and backward. However, for a script to do this, it must get permission from the avatar. This is done with the **run_time_permissions** event handler. This event handler is shown here.

```
run_time_permissions(integer perm)
{
    if (perm)
    {
        llTakeControls(CONTROL_FWD | CONTROL_BACK |
        CONTROL_DOWN | CONTROL_UP | CONTROL_RIGHT |
    CONTROL_LEFT | CONTROL_ROT_RIGHT |
        CONTROL_ROT_LEFT, TRUE, FALSE);
    }
}
```

The same event handler is used for all of the vehicles in this chapter.

Sitting Down as the Driver

When an avatar sits down to drive the car, the car must perform a setup before the avatar can begin driving the car. The **changed** event handler is called when an avatar sits on an object. First, the changed event handler checks to see whether it was called because an object was linked to it. In this case, it was the avatar that was linked to the car object.

```
changed(integer change)
{
    if (change & CHANGED_LINK)
    {
```

Next, the script checks to see what avatar sat on it. If it was an avatar that sat on the car, the car checks to see whether the avatar is the car's owner.

```
        key agent = llAvatarOnSitTarget();
        if (agent)
        {
```

```
if (agent != llGetOwner())
{
```

If it is not the car's owner, the car informs the avatar that they are not allowed to drive the car. The avatar is pushed away.

```
llSay(0, not_owner_message);
llUnSit(agent);
llPushObject(agent, <0,0,50>,
        ZERO_VECTOR, FALSE);
}
```

If it is the car's owner, it is time to set up the car so that it can be driven. First, the **car_start** sound is played. The car is then enabled as a physical object. A physical object can be pushed by external or internal forces. Permission to take the controls is then requested. Finally, the **car_run** sound is looped.

```
else
{
        llTriggerSound("car_start",1);
        llSleep(.4);
    llSetStatus(STATUS_PHYSICS, TRUE);
        llSleep(.1);
        llRequestPermissions(agent,
PERMISSION_TRIGGER_ANIMATION | PERMISSION_TAKE_CONTROLS);

        llLoopSound("car_run",1);
}
}
```

If the avatar is getting up, stop the sound and turn off physics. Controls are released. If physics are left on, any avatar who bumped into the parked car would move it.

```
else
{
    llStopSound();

    llSetStatus(STATUS_PHYSICS, FALSE);
    llSleep(.1);
    llSleep(.4);
    llReleaseControls();
    llTargetOmega(<0,0,0>,PI,0);
    llResetScript();
}
}
}
```

The call to **llTargetOmega** is very important. Without this call, the parked car will sometimes begin to rotate. This is a strange and undesirable effect.

Controlling the Car

The control event handler is called when the user interacts with the control keys. The control keys are the cursor keys and page up/down, as well as other control keys. The car will only use the cursor keys.

Vehicles in Second Life are moved by two motors; the linear motor and the angular motor. The linear motor can move the vehicle in any direction in the x, y and z coordinate planes. The angular motor can rotate the object in any of the x, y and z coordinate planes. The car uses both motors. The linear motor moves the car forwards and backwards. The angular motor turns the car.

The **control** event handler begins by setting up some variables that will be needed by the handler. Because cars turn differently when in reverse, a flag is required to indicate if we are in reverse. Also, a variable is created to hold the direction of the angular motor.

```
control(key id, integer level, integer edge)
{
    integer reverse=1;
    vector angular_motor;
```

The current speed is obtained. This will be used with turning. Cars need to be in motion to turn.

```
    //get current speed
    vector vel = llGetVel();
    float speed = llVecMag(vel);
```

Next, each of the relevant controls will be checked. The first control to be checked is the forward control. When the user presses forward, the linear motor is used to apply the force to move the car forward. Note also that the car is moving forward by setting the reverse variable to one.

```
    //car controls
    if(level & CONTROL_FWD)
    {
        llSetVehicleVectorParam(
    VEHICLE_LINEAR_MOTOR_DIRECTION, <forward_power,0,0>);
        reverse=1;
    }
```

If the user presses back, apply power in the opposite direction. Note also that the car has been put in reverse by setting the reverse variable to -1.

```
    if(level & CONTROL_BACK)
```

```
        {
                llSetVehicleVectorParam(
        VEHICLE_LINEAR_MOTOR_DIRECTION, <reverse_power,0,0>);
                reverse = -1;
        }
```

For a right turn, rotate the car in the z-coordinate. Rotate by the specified angle and take into account whether the car is going in reverse.

```
        if(level & (CONTROL_RIGHT|CONTROL_ROT_RIGHT))
        {
                angular_motor.z -= speed /
                        turning_ratio * reverse;
        }
```

For a left turn, rotate the car in the z-coordinate. Rotate by the specified angle and take into account whether the car is going in reverse.

```
        if(level & (CONTROL_LEFT|CONTROL_ROT_LEFT))
        {
                angular_motor.z += speed /
                        turning_ratio * reverse;
        }
```

Now the angular motor can be set.

```
        llSetVehicleVectorParam(
                VEHICLE_ANGULAR_MOTOR_DIRECTION, angular_motor);


}
```

The **control** event handler in the script is different for each vehicle type. This is because each vehicle handles differently. However, each vehicle shares some similarity in the **control** event handler.

Initializing the Car

The **state_entry** event handler initializes the car. Initialization is very different for each vehicle type. The car begins by setting the sit text and sit target.

```
    state_entry()
    {
        llSetSitText(sit_message);
        // forward-back,left-right,updown
        llSitTarget(<0.2,0,0.45>, ZERO_ROTATION );
```

Next, the camera is placed. The camera is offset behind and above the car. Now the camera looks into the car.

```
        llSetCameraEyeOffset(<-8, 0.0, 5.0>);
```

```
llSetCameraAtOffset(<1.0, 0.0, 2.0>);
```

The two sounds that are used are preloaded. This prevents any pause when the sounds are played for the first time.

```
llPreloadSound("car_start");
llPreloadSound("car_run");
```

Next the vehicle parameters are set. The first is the vehicle type, which is set by calling **llSetVehicleType**. Valid values for **llSetVehicleType** are listed in Table 10.1.

Table 10.1: Vehicle Types

Vehicle Type	Purpose
VEHICLE_TYPE_NONE	Not a vehicle.
VEHICLE_TYPE_SLED	Simple vehicle that bumps along the ground, has a tendency to move along its local x-axis.
VEHICLE_TYPE_CAR	Vehicle that bounces along the ground but requires motors to be driven from external controls or other source.
VEHICLE_TYPE_BOAT	Hovers over water with a great deal of friction and some angular deflection.
VEHICLE_TYPE_AIRPLANE	Uses linear deflection for lift, no hover, and must bank to turn.
VEHICLE_TYPE_BALLOON	Hover, and friction, and no deflection.

Additionally vehicle parameters are set using the **llSetVehicleFloatParam**, **llSetVehicleVectorParam** and **llSetVehicleRotationParam** function calls. Table 10.2 summarizes the values that can be set with the **llSetVehicleFloatParam**.

Table 10.2: Floating Point Vehicle Parameters

Parameter	Purpose
VEHICLE_ANGULAR_DEFLECTION_EFFICIENCY	Value between 0 (no deflection) and 1 (maximum strength).
VEHICLE_ANGULAR_DEFLECTION_TIMESCALE	Exponential timescale for the vehicle to achieve full angular deflection.

VEHICLE_ANGULAR_MOTOR_DECAY_TIMESCALE	Exponential timescale for the angular motor's effectiveness to decay toward zero.
VEHICLE_ANGULAR_MOTOR_TIMESCALE	Exponential timescale for the vehicle to achieve its full angular motor velocity.
VEHICLE_BANKING_EFFICIENCY	Value between -1 (leans out of turns), 0 (no banking), and +1 (leans into turns).
VEHICLE_BANKING_MIX	Value between 0 (static banking) and 1 (dynamic banking).
VEHICLE_BANKING_TIMESCALE	Exponential timescale for the banking behavior to take full effect.
VEHICLE_BUOYANCY	Value between -1 (double-gravity) and 1 (full anti-gravity).
VEHICLE_HOVER_HEIGHT	Height at which the vehicle will try to hover.
VEHICLE_HOVER_EFFICIENCY	Value between 0 (bouncy) and 1 (critically damped) hover behavior.
VEHICLE_HOVER_TIMESCALE	The period of time for the vehicle to achieve its hover height.
VEHICLE_LINEAR_DEFLECTION_EFFICIENCY	Value between 0 (no deflection) and 1 (maximum strength).
VEHICLE_LINEAR_DEFLECTION_TIMESCALE	An exponential timescale for the vehicle to redirect its velocity along its x-axis.
VEHICLE_LINEAR_MOTOR_DECAY_TIMESCALE	An exponential timescale for the linear motor's effectiveness to decay toward zero.
VEHICLE_LINEAR_MOTOR_TIMESCALE	An exponential timescale for the vehicle to achieve its full linear motor velocity.
VEHICLE_VERTICAL_ATTRACTION_EFFICIENCY	Value between 0 (bouncy) and 1 (critically damped) attraction of vehicle z-axis to world z-axis (vertical).

VEHICLE_VERTICAL_ATTRACTION_TIMESCALE	An exponential timescale for the vehicle to align its z-axis to the world z-axis (vertical).

The values that can be set with **llSetVehicleVectorParam** function are summarized in Table 10.3.

Table 10.3: Vector Vehicle Parameters

Parameter	Purpose
VEHICLE_ANGULAR_FRICTION_TIMESCALE	The vector of timescales for exponential decay of angular velocity about the three vehicle axes.
VEHICLE_ANGULAR_MOTOR_DIRECTION	The angular velocity that the vehicle will try to achieve.
VEHICLE_LINEAR_FRICTION_TIMESCALE	The vector of timescales for exponential decay of linear velocity along the three vehicle axes.
VEHICLE_LINEAR_MOTOR_DIRECTION	The linear velocity that the vehicle will try to achieve.
VEHICLE_LINEAR_MOTOR_OFFSET	The offset from the center of mass of the vehicle where the linear motor is applied.

The settings for the vehicle parameters of the car will now be reviewed. First, the vehicle type is set to car. Angular deflection is the tendency of a vehicle to move in certain directions. For example, a car will not tend to move in the z-coordinate (up and down). The angular deflection efficiency determines how effective angular deflection is. A value of 0.2 specifies angular deflection at 20%. This allows the car to turn fairly easily.

```
llSetVehicleType(VEHICLE_TYPE_CAR);
llSetVehicleFloatParam(
VEHICLE_ANGULAR_DEFLECTION_EFFICIENCY, 0.2);
```

A value of 0.8 specifies that linear deflection has 80% power. This means it takes more effort for the car to change its linear velocity.

```
llSetVehicleFloatParam(
```

```
VEHICLE_LINEAR_DEFLECTION_EFFICIENCY, 0.80);
```

It takes the car one tenth of a second for both linear and angular deflection to commence.

```
llSetVehicleFloatParam(
VEHICLE_ANGULAR_DEFLECTION_TIMESCALE, 0.10);
llSetVehicleFloatParam(
VEHICLE_LINEAR_DEFLECTION_TIMESCALE, 0.10);
```

It takes one second for the linear motor to reach full power.

```
llSetVehicleFloatParam(
VEHICLE_LINEAR_MOTOR_TIMESCALE, 1.0);
```

The linear motor will drop off in one fifth of a second. The car will not coast well.

```
llSetVehicleFloatParam(
VEHICLE_LINEAR_MOTOR_DECAY_TIMESCALE, 0.2);
```

The angular motor will reach full power in one tenth of a second.

```
llSetVehicleFloatParam(
VEHICLE_ANGULAR_MOTOR_TIMESCALE, 0.1);
```

The angular motor will drop off in 0.5 seconds. The car will stop turning fairly quickly when the user lets up on the control.

```
llSetVehicleFloatParam(
VEHICLE_ANGULAR_MOTOR_DECAY_TIMESCALE, 0.5);
```

Friction affects the car only in the y-coordinate, which is how the car moves forwards and backwards. The car can quickly fall or turn.

```
llSetVehicleVectorParam(
VEHICLE_LINEAR_FRICTION_TIMESCALE, <1000.0, 2.0, 1000.0>);
```

The car rotates fairly easily in the z-coordinate, but x and y are more difficult to rotate in.

```
llSetVehicleVectorParam(
VEHICLE_ANGULAR_FRICTION_TIMESCALE, <10.0, 10.0, 1000.0>);
```

A car should always stay right-side-up. The vertical attraction feature allows this.

```
llSetVehicleFloatParam(
VEHICLE_VERTICAL_ATTRACTION_EFFICIENCY, 0.50);
llSetVehicleFloatParam(
VEHICLE_VERTICAL_ATTRACTION_TIMESCALE, 0.50);
```

These values work well for a car. However, they will be considerably different for a boat or helicopter.

Who Sits Where

The car allows for one passenger, in addition to the driver. Additional passengers will be ejected. Figure 10.5 shows the car with a driver and one passenger.

Figure 10.5: A Car with Two Passengers

Extra seats must be provided to allow additional people, other than the driver to ride in a vehicle. The passenger seat has a simple **llSitTarget** function call in its **state_entry** event handler. The passenger seat can be seen here.

Listing 10.3: Car Passenger Seat (CarSeat.lsl)

```
default
{
    state_entry()
    {
        llSitTarget(<0.2,0,0.45>, ZERO_ROTATION );
    }
}
```

The driver's seat should be the root prim, which is the last prim selected. The passenger's seat should be the second to the last prim selected. A third script is also required, to disallow further seating. The third to the last prim selected should contain a script that prevents the user from sitting down. Such a script can be seen in Listing 10.4.

Listing 10.4: Can't Sit Here (DontSitHere.lsl)

```
default
{
    state_entry()
    {
        llSitTarget(<0.2,0,0.45>, ZERO_ROTATION );
    }

    changed(integer change)
    {
        if (change & CHANGED_LINK)
        {
            key agent = llAvatarOnSitTarget();
            if (agent)
            {
                llUnSit(agent);
                llSay(0,"Sorry, this vehicle is full.");
            }
        }
    }
}
```

The "don't sit here" script is needed because an avatar will try to choose a seat in the following order.

- If the exact prim selected can be sat on, choose it
- Next, try to sit on the root prim
- Next, try to sit on the prim selected just before the root prim
- Next, try to sit on the prim selected two before the root prim and so on

Because of this, the "chain" of sit targets must be broken just beyond the last passenger seat. The "do not sit here" script specifies a sit target in the **state_entry**, as for the passenger seat:

```
default
{
    state_entry()
    {
        llSitTarget(<0.2,0,0.45>, ZERO_ROTATION );
    }
```

Whenever the changed event handler is called, the avatar should be ejected with the **llUnSit** function call.

```
changed(integer change)
{
    if (change & CHANGED_LINK)
    {
        key agent = llAvatarOnSitTarget();
        if (agent)
        {
            llUnSit(agent);
            llSay(0,"Sorry, this vehicle is full.");
        }
    }
}
```

This prevents avatars from sitting on unintended parts of the vehicle.

Turning the Wheels

To appear more realistic, the car turns its wheels when in motion. There are several ways that this is commonly done in Second Life vehicles. The method used for this car is shown in Listing 10.5.

Listing 10.5: Car Wheel (WheelScript.lsl)

```
default
{
    state_entry()
    {
        llSetTimerEvent(0.20);
    }
    timer()
    {
        vector vel = llGetVel();
        float speed = llVecMag(vel);
        if(speed > 0)
        {
            llSetTextureAnim(ANIM_ON | SMOOTH | LOOP, 0, 0, 0,
            0, 1, speed*0.5);
        }
        else
        {
            llSetTextureAnim(ANIM_ON | SMOOTH | LOOP | REVERSE,
            0, 0, 0, 0, 1, speed*0.5);
        }
    }
```

```
}
```

The above script is contained in all four wheels of the car. The script works by rotating the texture of the wheel in one direction when the car is moving forward, and in another direction when moving backwards. The speed of the car can be obtained by calling **llGetVel**, as seen here.

```
vector vel = llGetVel();
float speed = llVecMag(vel);
if(speed > 0)
{
     llSetTextureAnim(ANIM_ON | SMOOTH | LOOP, 0, 0, 0, 0, 1,
          speed*0.5);
}
else
{
     llSetTextureAnim(ANIM_ON | SMOOTH | LOOP | REVERSE, 0, 0,
          0, 0, 1, speed*0.5);
}
```

The hubcaps must be rotated too. However, they need to be rotated along a different coordinate than the tires. Other than that, their script is identical to the wheel script. The hubcap script is shown in Listing 10.6.

Listing 10.6: Rotate the Hubcaps (WheelScript.lsl)

```
default
{
    state_entry()
    {
        llSetTimerEvent(0.20);
    }
    timer()
    {
        vector vel = llGetVel();
        float speed = llVecMag(vel);
        if(speed > 0)
        {
            llSetTextureAnim(ANIM_ON | SMOOTH | LOOP, 0, 0, 0,
            0, 1, speed*0.5);
        }
        else
        {
            llSetTextureAnim(ANIM_ON | SMOOTH | LOOP | REVERSE,
            0, 0, 0, 0, 1, speed*0.5);
        }
    }
}
```

There are quite a few parts to the car. Unlike previous examples, one script can not handle the entire object. Individual scripts are needed in several of the prims that make up the car. Some parts of the scripts will be reused in other vehicles. However, the other vehicles in this chapter are either air or sea based. This introduces some differences from the land based car.

Summary

Objects in Second Life can be moved either physically or non-physically. Chapter 9 showed how to move objects non-physically. This chapter showed how to move objects physically. When objects are moved physically, force is applied to the object to cause movement.

Before force can be applied to an object, the object must be marked as physical. This can be done in two ways. First, the physical checkbox can be clicked in the object properties. Second, the physical property of an object can be changed programatically.

There are many attributes of objects that can be altered as a script runs. A script can resize objects, change textures or alter many other attributes of the object. The next chapter will show how scripts can be used to alter objects.

CHAPTER 11: CHANGING OBJECT ATTRIBUTES

- Changing a Primitive's Attributes
- Reading a Primitive's Attributes
- Modifying a Linked Primitive's Attributes

It is also possible to modify a primitive that is either running the active script, or linked to the active script. This allows any of the attributes, seen when you edit a prim, to be modified by the script. These attributes allow you to change such things as the color, texture and size of a prim as well as many other attributes.

To set attributes for the prim that holds the script, use the **llSetPrimitiveParams** function. To set the attributes for a prim that is linked, use the **llSetLinkPrimitiveParams** function.

Using llSetPrimitiveParams

The signature for the **llSetPrimitiveParams** is very simple, as seen here.

```
llSetPrimitiveParams(list rule)
```

Do not let the somewhat simple format of the signature fool you. The **llSetPrimitiveParams** function is one of the most complex functions in the Linden Scripting Language. The list that is passed in defines what attributes are to be set. For example, to set the color of a prim, the following call would be used.

```
llSetPrimitiveParams( [PRIM_COLOR, ALL_SIDES, <1, 1, 1>, 0.75]  )
```

The above call sets all sides of the prim to white. The value **<1,1,1>** specifies white because the value one specifies full intensity for red, green and blue. The values for red, green and blue can range between zero and one. Using these values allows any color to be specified. The value 0.75 specifies the transparency of the prim. A value of zero is completely non-transparent, where a value of one is invisible.

The format of the list is a constant, that defines what attribute to set, followed by whatever additional values that constant is defined to deal with. In the above example, the **PRIM_COLOR** constant is capable of handling three parameters. As a result, the list contains four values.

It is also possible to set two attributes with one call to **llSetPrimitiveParams**. Simply concatenate two constants, and their parameters, together. For example, to set both the color and size of a prim, use the following function call.

```
llSetPrimitiveParams( [PRIM_COLOR, ALL_SIDES, <1, 1, 1>, 0.75],
[PRIM_SIZE, < 10, 10, 10>]  )
```

There are many different constants that can be used with the list. Table 11.1 summarizes all of the constants that can be used with **llSetPrimitiveParams**.

Table 11.1: Constants for llSetPrimitiveParams

Constant Name	Description	Parameter(s)	Example Rule
PRIM_BUMP_SHINY	Sets bumpmapping and shininess of a face	integer face, PRIM_SHINY_xxx, PRIM_BUMP_xxx	[PRIM_BUMP_SHINY, 2, PRIM_SHINY_LOW, PRIM_BUMP_GRAVEL]
PRIM_COLOR	Sets color and alpha of a face	integer face, vector color, float alpha	[PRIM_COLOR, 1, <1, 0, 0>, 0.75]
PRIM_FLEXIBLE	Toggles flexible property and attributes: softness, gravity, drag (friction), wind, tension, and force.	boolean flexible, integer softness, float gravity, float friction, float wind, float tension, vector force	[PRIM_FLEXIBLE, TRUE, 2, 0.3, 2.0, 0.0, 1.0, <0, 0, 0>]
PRIM_FULL-BRIGHT	Sets full bright of a face on or off.	integer face, boolean on	[PRIM_FULL-BRIGHT, ALL_SIDES, TRUE]
PRIM_MATERIAL	Sets material of the prim	PRIM_MATERIAL_xxx	[PRIM_MATERIAL, PRIM_MATERIAL_RUBBER]
PRIM_PHANTOM	Sets phantom property of an object	boolean phantom	[PRIM_PHANTOM, TRUE]
PRIM_PHYSICS	Sets physics property of an object	boolean physics	[PRIM_PHYSICS, TRUE]
PRIM_POINT_LIGHT	Toggles light property and attributes: color, intensity, radius, and falloff.	boolean on, vector color, float intensity, float radius, float falloff	[PRIM_POINT_LIGHT, TRUE, <1, 1, 1>, 1.0, 10.0, 0.75]
PRIM_POSITION	Moves object to position.	vector position	[PRIM_POSITION, <128, 128, 40>]
PRIM_ROTATION	Sets the rotation of the object	rotation rot	[PRIM_ROTATION, <0, 0, 0, 1>]

PRIM_SIZE	Sets the scale of an object (Between <0.01,0.01,0.01> and <10,10,10>)	vector size	[PRIM_SIZE, <4, 3, 0.1>]
PRIM_TEMP_ON_REZ	Sets temporary on rez property of an object	boolean temp_on_rez	[PRIM_TEMP_ON_REZ, TRUE]
PRIM_TYPE	Sets the basic prim type; will unsit all avatars on object.	See next table	See next table
PRIM_TEXGEN	Sets the texture mapping mode, either PRIM_TEX-GEN_DEFAULT or PRIM_TEXGEN_PLANAR.	integer face, integer type	[PRIM_TEXGEN, ALL_SIDES, PRIM_TEXGEN_DEFAULT]
PRIM_TEXTURE	Sets the texture properties of a face	integer face, string name, vector repeats, vector offsets, float rotation	[PRIM_TEXTURE, 0, "grass", <2,8,0>, <.5,.5,0>, PI / 4]

Several of the constants require additional constants to be specified. For example, the **PRIM_TYPE** constant allows the type of primitive to be changed. For example, you could change a box to a sphere. Table 11.2 summarizes all of the primitive types that can be specified, as well as their optional parameters.

Table 11.2: PRIM_TYPE Constants

Constant Name	Type	Parameter(s)	Example rule
PRIM_TYPE_BOX	Box	integer holeshape, vector cut, float hollow, vector twist, vector taper_b, vector topshear	[PRIM_TYPE, PRIM_TYPE_BOX, 0, <0.0, 1.0, 0.0>, 0.0, <0.0, 0.0, 0.0>, <1.0, 1.0, 0.0>, <0.0, 0.0, 0.0>]
PRIM_TYPE_CYL-INDER	Cylinder	integer holeshape, vector cut, float hollow, vector twist, vector taper_b, vector topshear	[PRIM_TYPE, PRIM_TYPE_CYL-INDER, 0, <0.0, 1.0, 0.0>, 0.0, <0.0, 0.0, 0.0>, <1.0, 1.0, 0.0>, <0.0, 0.0, 0.0>]

PRIM_TYPE_ PRISM	Prism	integer holeshape, vector cut, float hollow, vector twist, vector taper_b, vector topshear	[PRIM_TYPE, PRIM_TYPE_ PRISM, 0, <0.0, 1.0, 0.0>, 0.0, <0.0, 0.0, 0.0>, <0.0, 0.0, 0.0>, <0.0, 0.0, 0.0>]
PRIM_TYPE_ SPHERE	Sphere	integer holeshape, vector cut, float hollow, vector twist, vector dimple	[PRIM_TYPE, PRIM_TYPE_ SPHERE, 0, <0.0, 1.0, 0.0>, 0.0, <0.0, 0.0, 0.0>, <0.0, 1.0, 0.0>]
PRIM_TYPE_TO- RUS	Torus	integer holeshape, vector cut, float hollow, vector twist, vector holesize, vector topshear, vector profilecut, vector taper_a, float revolutions, float radiusoffset, float skew	[PRIM_TYPE, PRIM_TYPE_TO-RUS, 0, <0.0, 1.0, 0.0>, 0.0, <0.0, 0.0, 0.0>, <1.0, 0.25, 0.0>, <0.0, 0.0, 0.0>, <0.0, 1.0, 0.0>, <0.0, 0.0, 0.0>, 1.0, 0.0, 0.0]
PRIM_TYPE_ TUBE	Tube	integer holeshape, vector cut, float hollow, vector twist, vector holesize, vector topshear, vector profilecut, vector taper_a, float revolutions, float radiusoffset, float skew	[PRIM_TYPE, PRIM_TYPE_ TUBE, 0, <0.0, 1.0, 0.0>, 0.0, <0.0, 0.0, 0.0>, <1.0, 0.25, 0.0>, <0.0, 0.0, 0.0>, <0.0, 1.0, 0.0>, <0.0, 0.0, 0.0>, 1.0, 0.0, 0.0]
PRIM_TYPE_ RING	Ring	integer holeshape, vector cut, float hollow, vector twist, vector holesize, vector topshear, vector profilecut, vector taper_a, float revolutions, float radiusoffset, float skew	[PRIM_TYPE, PRIM_TYPE_ RING, 0, <0.0, 1.0, 0.0>, 0.0, <0.0, 0.0, 0.0>, <1.0, 0.25, 0.0>, <0.0, 0.0, 0.0>, <0.0, 1.0, 0.0>, <0.0, 0.0, 0.0>, 1.0, 0.0, 0.0]

Note: Some restrictions apply to the above primitive types. Specifically, their parameters must adhere to:

- repeats - x and y range from 0.0 to 100 (z is ignored).
- offsets - x and y range from -1 to 1 (z is ignored).
- cut/dimple/profilecut - x and y range from 0.0 to 1.0, x must be at least 0.05 smaller than y (z is ignored).
- hollow - ranges from 0.0 (solid) to 0.95 (maximum hollowed).
- Twist – only with boxes, cylinders and prisms boxes, cylinders, prisms - ranges from -0.5 (-180 degree in the edit window) to 0.5 (+180 degree in the edit window) for both x and y (z is ignored)
- Twist with spheres, tubes and torus rings - ranges from -1.0 (-360 degree in the edit window) to 1.0 (+360 degree in the edit window) for both x and y (z is ignored)
- Holesize - x ranges from 0.05 to 1.0, and y ranges from 0.05 (large hole) to 0.50 (no hole)
- taper_b - ranges from 0.0 to 2.0 for both x and y (z is ignored)
- topshear - ranges from -0.5 to 0.5 for both x and y (z is ignored)
- taper_a - ranges from -1.0 to 1.0 for both x and y (z is ignored)
- revolutions - ranges from 1.0 to 4.00
- radiusoffset - depends on holesize y and revolutions

When a hole is specified for a prim, the shape of the hole can also be specified. Table 11.3 lists the constants used to specify the shape of the hole.

Table 11.3: Holeshape Constants

Constant	Shape
PRIM_HOLE_DEFAULT	default (matches the prim type: square for box, circle for cylinder, etc.)
PRIM_HOLE_SQUARE	square
PRIM_HOLE_CIRCLE	circle
PRIM_HOLE_TRIANGLE	triangle

Prims are completely smooth by default. It is possible to create "bumpy" prims. These have a slight 3D texture on their surface. There are several types of bumps that are allowed. Table 11.4 lists the bumpy constants.

Table 11.4: Bumpmapping Constants

Constant	Description
PRIM_BUMP_NONE	none: no bump map

PRIM_BUMP_BRIGHT	brightness: generate bump map from highlights
PRIM_BUMP_DARK	darkness: generate bump map from lowlights
PRIM_BUMP_WOOD	woodgrain
PRIM_BUMP_BARK	bark
PRIM_BUMP_BRICKS	bricks
PRIM_BUMP_CHECKER	checker
PRIM_BUMP_CONCRETE	concrete
PRIM_BUMP_TILE	crustytile
PRIM_BUMP_STONE	cutstone: blocks
PRIM_BUMP_DISKS	discs: packed circles
PRIM_BUMP_GRAVEL	gravel
PRIM_BUMP_BLOBS	petridish: blobby amoeba-like shapes
PRIM_BUMP_SIDING	siding
PRIM_BUMP_LARGETILE	stonetile
PRIM_BUMP_STUCCO	stucco
PRIM_BUMP_SUCTION	suction: rings
PRIM_BUMP_WEAVE	weave

Shininess is the degree to which a prim reflects light. There are several levels of shininess that can be specified in Second Life. Table 11.5 lists these shininess levels.

Table 11.5: Shininess Constants

Constant	Description
PRIM_SHINY_NONE	none
PRIM_SHINY_LOW	low
PRIM_SHINY_MEDIUM	medium
PRIM_SHINY_HIGH	high

Prims can be made of a specific material. These material types only matter if the prim is "physical". Physical prims were discussed in Chapter 10. Material types define the friction and mass of an object. The default material type is wood. The majority of the Second Life world is made of wood as many builders simply leave the material set to wood. The material types are summarized in Table 11.6.

Table 11.6: Material Constants

Constant	Description
PRIM_MATERIAL_STONE	stone
PRIM_MATERIAL_METAL	metal
PRIM_MATERIAL_GLASS	glass
PRIM_MATERIAL_WOOD	wood
PRIM_MATERIAL_FLESH	flesh
PRIM_MATERIAL_PLASTIC	plastic
PRIM_MATERIAL_RUBBER	rubber

As you can see, there are a considerable number of options to be used with **llSetPrimitiveParams**. The tables presented above can provide a quick look-up for exactly the attribute that you would like to set.

In addition to **llSetPrimitiveParams**, there are other functions provided by the Linden Scripting Language that also use many of the constants defined in the preceding tables. The function **llGetPrimitiveParams** retrieves information about an attribute. The **llSetLinkPrimitiveParam** function allows attributes to be set for a linked prim. These functions will now be described.

Using llGetPrimitiveParams

It is also possible to retrieve information about a prim using the constants defined earlier in this chapter. To do this, use the **llGetPrimitiveParams** function. The **llGetPrimitiveParams** function is shown here.

```
list llGetPrimitiveParams(list params)
```

Simply pass **llGetPrimitiveParams** a list of the attributes to be obtained. For example, to retrieve the size of a prim, use the following code.

```
list size = llGetPrimitiveParams( [PRIM_SIZE] );
```

This will store the size to the list named size. To retrieve the size as a **vector**, use the following code.

```
vector v = (vector)llList2String(size,0);
```

To restore the size of a primitive, using the size list, use the following code.

```
llSetPrimitiveParams( [PRIM_SIZE] + size );
```

So far, all of the operations performed have been on the same prim that contains the script. It is also possible to set the attributes for linked prims as well. This technique is covered in the next section.

Using llSetLinkPrimitiveParams

A Second Life object is made up of a collection of prims. These prims are linked together and are called a link set. The last prim linked becomes the root prim. The root prim is the primitive whose x, y and z position and rotation values define the position and rotation for the entire object. Usually, the script for the entire object is placed in the root prim.

The **llSetLinkPrimitiveParams** function can be used to set attributes for both the root prim, and any linked prims. The signature for the **llSetLinkPrimitiveParams** function is shown here.

```
llSetLinkPrimitiveParams(integer linknumber, list rules)
```

As you can see, the signature for **llSetLinkPrimitiveParams** is very similar to **llSetPrimitiveParams**. The only difference is that a link number is passed in. This specifies which member of the link set to set the attributes for. The first element is the root prim, the second is the second prim after the root prim, and so on.

Setting Attribute Properties

In this section, an example script will be presented that makes use of the **llSetPrimitiveParams** function. This script will implement a simple cube that randomly changes colors every ten seconds. This script is shown in Listing 11.1.

Listing 11.1: Random Color Cube

```
default
{
    state_entry()
    {
        llSetTimerEvent(10);
    }

    timer()
    {
        float red = llFrand(1);
        float green = llFrand(1);
        float blue = llFrand(1);

        vector color = <red,green,blue>;

        llSetPrimitiveParams( [PRIM_COLOR, ALL_SIDES, color, 1]
            );

    }
}
```

This script begins by setting a timer event that will occur every ten seconds. Each time the timer event is called, three random values are generated for red, green and blue. These components are combined in a vector to produce a color. This color is then applied to the prim.

In previous chapters functions such as **llSetPos** and **llGetPos** were presented to change the position of a primitive. You may be wondering when you should use a specialized function such as **llSetPos** and when you should use the generic **llSetPrimitiveParams**. The choice as yours, as they both accomplish the same thing. Generally, the specialized versions such as **llSetPos**, have slightly higher performance, since a list is not need to be created. However, not all attributes have specialized accessor functions. For many of the attributes **llSetPrimitiveParams** is the only way to set these attributes.

Summary

This chapter showed how to set the individual attributes of prims. There are many different attributes defined for a primitive. Usually these primitives are set when the prim is first built in Second Life. However, all of these attributes can be set programatically. This is done using the **llSetPrimitiveParams** function.

Additionally, the current state of any of these attributes can be obtained using the **llGetPrimitiveParams** function. The **llSetPrimitiveParmas** function always operates on the prim that contains the current script. It is also possible to use the **llSetLinkPrimitiveParams** function set the attributes for other primitives in the current link set.

Primitives and objects are not the only items visible in Second Life. Particles are also an important part of the Second Life world. Particles are simple 2D sprites that have no physical properties. They are often used for smoke or to make objects shine or glow. The next chapter will over particles.

CHAPTER 12: USING PARTICLES

- The Basic Particle Emitter
- Creating a Fog Machine
- Using a Snow Machine

Any prim in Second Life can emit particles. Particles are 2D sprites emitted from their prim in definable ways. Particles are not objects in the sense that they can be touched or count against the land's maximum object count. Particles are generated completely on the client side, so they do not contribute to in-game lag. However, they can cause some lag to the client computer viewing them.

Particle emitters are used for a wide range of purposes in Second Life. Some of their uses include:

- Creating insects and leaves in landscaped areas
- Creating flashy laser type effects in clubs
- Leaving smoke and wave trails behind vehicles
- Causing jewelry to sparkle
- Smoke from chimneys
- Creating explosions

This chapter provides several examples for particle emitters. The first example shows a basic particle emitter script. This will be the starting point for all other examples.

Basic Particle Emitter

The basic particle emitter script shown in this recipe emits red particles that float upward. The basic particle emitter is designed to be a starting point from which other particle emitters can be created. Most of the particle emitters in this chapter used the basic particle emitter as a starting point. The basic particle emitter can be seen in action in Figure 12.1.

Figure 12.1: Basic Particle Emitter

The script for the basic particle emitter can be seen in Listing 12.1.

Listing 12.1: Basic Particle Emitter

```
generalParticleEmitterOn()
{
    llParticleSystem([
        PSYS_PART_FLAGS , 0
    //| PSYS_PART_BOUNCE_MASK        //Bounce on object's z-axis
      | PSYS_PART_WIND_MASK          //Particles are moved by wind
      | PSYS_PART_INTERP_COLOR_MASK  //Colors fade from start to
end
      | PSYS_PART_INTERP_SCALE_MASK  //Scale fades from beginning
to end
      | PSYS_PART_FOLLOW_SRC_MASK    //Particles follow the emitter
      | PSYS_PART_FOLLOW_VELOCITY_MASK//Particles are created at the
velocity of the emitter
    //| PSYS_PART_TARGET_POS_MASK    //Particles follow the target
      | PSYS_PART_EMISSIVE_MASK      //Particles are self-lit
(glow)
```

```
    //| PSYS_PART_TARGET_LINEAR_MASK//Undocumented--Sends parti-
cles in straight line?
    ,

    //PSYS_SRC_TARGET_KEY , NULL_KEY,//The particles will head to-
wards the specified key
    //Select one of the following for a pattern:
    //PSYS_SRC_PATTERN_DROP                Particles start at
emitter with no velocity
    //PSYS_SRC_PATTERN_EXPLODE             Particles explode from
the emitter
    //PSYS_SRC_PATTERN_ANGLE               Particles are emitted
in a 2-D angle
    //PSYS_SRC_PATTERN_ANGLE_CONE          Particles are emitted
in a 3-D cone
    //PSYS_SRC_PATTERN_ANGLE_CONE_EMPTY    Particles are emitted
everywhere except for a 3-D cone

    PSYS_SRC_PATTERN,              PSYS_SRC_PATTERN_ANGLE_CONE

    ,PSYS_SRC_TEXTURE,            ""           //UUID of the de-
sired particle texture, or inventory name
    ,PSYS_SRC_MAX_AGE,           0.0          //Time, in sec-
onds, for particles to be emitted. 0 = forever
    ,PSYS_PART_MAX_AGE,          4.0          //Lifetime, in
seconds, that a particle lasts
    ,PSYS_SRC_BURST_RATE,        0.5          //How long, in
seconds, between each emission
    ,PSYS_SRC_BURST_PART_COUNT,  6            //Number of par-
ticles per emission
    ,PSYS_SRC_BURST_RADIUS,      10.0         //Radius of emis-
sion
    ,PSYS_SRC_BURST_SPEED_MIN,   .4           //Minimum speed of
an emitted particle
    ,PSYS_SRC_BURST_SPEED_MAX,   .5           //Maximum speed of
an emitted particle
    ,PSYS_SRC_ACCEL,             <0,0,1>   //Acceleration of par-
ticles each second
    ,PSYS_PART_START_COLOR,      <1,0,0> //Starting RGB color
    ,PSYS_PART_END_COLOR,        <1,0,0> //Ending RGB color, if
INTERP_COLOR_MASK is on
    ,PSYS_PART_START_ALPHA,      1.0          //Starting trans-
parency, 1 is opaque, 0 is transparent.
    ,PSYS_PART_END_ALPHA,        1.0          //Ending transpar-
ency
    ,PSYS_PART_START_SCALE,      <.25,.25,.25> //Starting par-
ticle size
```

```
     ,PSYS_PART_END_SCALE,            <1.5,1.5,1.5>  //Ending particle
size, if INTERP_SCALE_MASK is on
     ,PSYS_SRC_ANGLE_BEGIN,          300 * DEG_TO_RAD //Inner angle
for ANGLE patterns
     ,PSYS_SRC_ANGLE_END,            60 * DEG_TO_RAD//Outer angle for
ANGLE patterns
     ,PSYS_SRC_OMEGA,                <0.0,0.0,0.0>  //Rotation of
ANGLE patterns, similar to llTargetOmega()
             ]);
}

generalParticleEmitterOff()
{
    llParticleSystem([]);
}

default
{
    state_entry()
    {
        generalParticleEmitterOn();
    }

    touch_start( integer num )
    {
        // uncomment the following line to allow this effect
        // to be turned off
        //state off;
    }
}

state off
{
    state_entry()
    {
        generalParticleEmitterOff();
    }

    touch_start( integer num )
    {
        state default;
    }
}
```

Nearly all of the work of the basic particle emitter is performed by the call to in-side of the function.

Creating a Particle Emitter

A particle emitter is created by passing a list to the function. This works in a similar way to the function, which is also controlled by a list. This list is a series of name-value pairs. The majority of the code presented in Listing 12.1 creates this list.

The first name-value pair in the list is . This defines a number of flags that define how the particles behave. These flags can be combined using the bit-wise or opera-tor(|). These flags are summarized in Table 12.1.

Table 12.1: PSYS_PART_FLAGS Flags

Flag	Purpose
PSYS_PART_BOUNCE_MASK	Bounce on object's z-axis.
PSYS_PART_WIND_MASK	Particles are moved by wind.
PSYS_PART_INTERP_COLOR_MASK	Colors fade from start to end.
PSYS_PART_INTERP_SCALE_MASK	Scale fades from beginning to end.
PSYS_PART_FOLLOW_SRC_MASK	Particles follow the emitter.
PSYS_PART_FOLLOW_VELOCITY_MASK	Particles are created at the velocity of the emitter.
PSYS_PART_TARGET_POS_MASK	Particles follow the target.
PSYS_PART_EMISSIVE_MASK	Particles are self-lit (glow).
PSYS_PART_TARGET_LINEAR_MASK	Undocumented flag.

A particle system should specify a pattern using the name-value pair. Table 12.2 lists the possible patterns that can be specified.

Table 12.2: PSYS_SRC_PATTERN Values

Pattern	Purpose
PSYS_SRC_PATTERN_DROP	Particles start at emitter with no velocity.
PSYS_SRC_PATTERN_EXPLODE	Particles explode from the emitter.
PSYS_SRC_PATTERN_ANGLE	Particles are emitted in a 2-D angle.

PSYS_SRC_PATTERN_ANGLE_CONE	Particles are emitted in a 3-D cone.
PSYS_SRC_PATTERN_ANGLE_CONE_EMPTY	Particles are emitted everywhere except for a 3-D cone.

The remaining name-value pairs are simply a name and a simple value such as a number, texture key, or vector. These name-value pairs are summarized in Table 12.3.

Table 12.3: Remaining Particle Emitter Name-Value Pairs

Name-Value Pair	Purpose
PSYS_SRC_TARGET_KEY	Specifies the key of an object or avatar that the particles will move towards. The PSYS_PART_TARGET_POS_MASK flag must be specified for the PSYS_SRC_TARGET_KEY name-value pair to have any effect.
PSYS_SRC_TEXTURE	Specifies the UUID or inventory name of the desired particle texture.
PSYS_SRC_MAX_AGE	Specifies the maximum amount of time, in seconds, that the particle emitter should emit particles. Specify 0.0 for forever.
PSYS_PART_MAX_AGE	Specifies the amount of time, in seconds, that each particle should remain for.
PSYS_SRC_BURST_RATE	Specifies the amount of time, in seconds, between each emission of particles.
PSYS_SRC_BURST_PART_COUNT	Specifies the number of particles to be produced during each emission.
PSYS_SRC_BURST_RADIUS	Specifies the radius, in meters, of each particle emission.
PSYS_SRC_BURST_SPEED_MIN	Specifies the minimum burst speed of the particles.
PSYS_SRC_BURST_SPEED_MAX	Specifies the maximum burst speed of the particles.
PSYS_SRC_ACCEL	Specifies the acceleration vector for the particles.
PSYS_PART_START_COLOR	Specifies a starting RGB color for the particles. Only works if the INTERP_COLOR_MASK flag is on.

PSYS_PART_END_COLOR,	Specifies an ending RGB color for the particles. Only works if the INTERP_COLOR_MASK flag is on.
PSYS_PART_START_ALPHA	Specifies the starting transparency for particles. Specify a value of 1.0 for opaque and 0.0 for transparent.
PSYS_PART_END_ALPHA	Specifies the ending transparency for particles. Specify a value of 1.0 for opaque and 0.0 for transparent.
PSYS_PART_START_SCALE	Specifies the starting particle size, as a vector. Only works if the INTERP_SCALE_MASK flag was set.
PSYS_PART_END_SCALE	Specifies the ending particle size, as a vector. Only works if the INTERP_SCALE_MASK flag was set.
PSYS_SRC_ANGLE_BEGIN	Specifies the inner angle, in radians, for angle patterns.
PSYS_SRC_ANGLE_END	Specifies the outer angle, in radians, for angle patterns.
PSYS_SRC_OMEGA	Specifies the angle of rotation patterns.

By modifying these values, any sort of particle emitter script can be created. The basic particle emitter script presented in this example creates red particles. The script specifies a vector of for the and . The value is RGB for red. The particles start with a size of and end with a size of . No texture is specified so the particles will be glowing spheres. To cause the particles to go up, a of is specified.

Many of the remaining examples in this chapter will simply modify the values of the basic particle script to create other effects. Once a particle system has been specified for a prim, that prim will continue to emit particles until the amount of time specified by elapses. If a value of zero was specified, the prim will continue to create particles indefinably. To stop the prim from producing particles, the function call should be called with an empty set, as seen here:

```
llParticleSystem([]);
```

Once an empty set has been specified to the particle system, no more particles will be produced.

A Fog Machine

There are many different effects that can be achieved with a particle emitter. One of the most common is a fog machine. A fog machine produces a fog effect all around the device. Figure 12.2 shows a fog machine in operation.

Figure 12.2: A Fog Machine

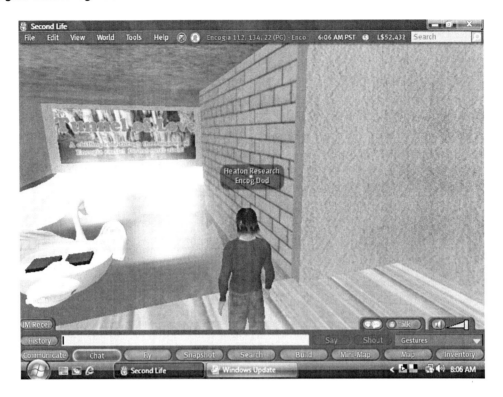

The fog machine was built using the particle emitter script shown in Listing 12.1. The fog machine can be seen in Listing 12.2.

Listing 12.2: A Fog Machine

```
generalParticleEmitterOn()
{
    llParticleSystem([
        PSYS_PART_FLAGS , 0
    //| PSYS_PART_BOUNCE_MASK          //Bounce on object's z-axis
    //| PSYS_PART_WIND_MASK             //Particles are moved by
wind
      | PSYS_PART_INTERP_COLOR_MASK   //Colors fade from start to
end
      | PSYS_PART_INTERP_SCALE_MASK   //Scale fades from beginning
to end
      | PSYS_PART_FOLLOW_SRC_MASK     //Particles follow the emitter
      | PSYS_PART_FOLLOW_VELOCITY_MASK//Particles are created at the
velocity of the emitter
    //| PSYS_PART_TARGET_POS_MASK      //Particles follow the target
      | PSYS_PART_EMISSIVE_MASK       //Particles are self-lit
```

```
(glow)
    //| PSYS_PART_TARGET_LINEAR_MASK//Undocumented--Sends parti-
cles in straight line?

    ,

    //PSYS_SRC_TARGET_KEY , NULL_KEY,//The particles will head to-
wards the specified key
    //Select one of the following for a pattern:
    //PSYS_SRC_PATTERN_DROP              Particles start at
emitter with no velocity
    //PSYS_SRC_PATTERN_EXPLODE           Particles explode from
the emitter
    //PSYS_SRC_PATTERN_ANGLE             Particles are emitted
in a 2-D angle
    //PSYS_SRC_PATTERN_ANGLE_CONE        Particles are emitted
in a 3-D cone
    //PSYS_SRC_PATTERN_ANGLE_CONE_EMPTY  Particles are emitted
everywhere except for a 3-D cone

    PSYS_SRC_PATTERN,              PSYS_SRC_PATTERN_ANGLE_CONE

    ,PSYS_SRC_TEXTURE,             ""            //UUID of the de-
sired particle texture, or inventory name
    ,PSYS_SRC_MAX_AGE,            0.0           //Time, in sec-
onds, for particles to be emitted. 0 = forever
    ,PSYS_PART_MAX_AGE,           10.0          //Lifetime, in
seconds, that a particle lasts
    ,PSYS_SRC_BURST_RATE,         0.2           //How long, in
seconds, between each emission
    ,PSYS_SRC_BURST_PART_COUNT,   2             //Number of par-
ticles per emission
    ,PSYS_SRC_BURST_RADIUS,       10.0          //Radius of emis-
sion
    ,PSYS_SRC_BURST_SPEED_MIN,    .1            //Minimum speed of
an emitted particle
    ,PSYS_SRC_BURST_SPEED_MAX,    .1            //Maximum speed of
an emitted particle
    ,PSYS_SRC_ACCEL,              <0,0,0.05>    //Acceleration of
particles each second
    ,PSYS_PART_START_COLOR,       <1,1,1> //Starting RGB color
    ,PSYS_PART_END_COLOR,         <1,1,1> //Ending RGB color, if
INTERP_COLOR_MASK is on
    ,PSYS_PART_START_ALPHA,       0.1           //Starting trans-
parency, 1 is opaque, 0 is transparent.
    ,PSYS_PART_END_ALPHA,         0.1           //Ending transpar-
ency
    ,PSYS_PART_START_SCALE,       <15,15,15> //Starting particle
```

```
size
    ,PSYS_PART_END_SCALE,           <5,5,5>  //Ending particle size,
if INTERP_SCALE_MASK is on
    ,PSYS_SRC_ANGLE_BEGIN,          0 * DEG_TO_RAD //Inner angle for
ANGLE patterns
    ,PSYS_SRC_ANGLE_END,            360 * DEG_TO_RAD//Outer angle for
ANGLE patterns
    ,PSYS_SRC_OMEGA,                <0.0,0.0,0.0>  //Rotation of
ANGLE patterns, similar to llTargetOmega()
            ]);
}

generalParticleEmitterOff()
{
    llParticleSystem([]);
}

default
{
    state_entry()
    {
        generalParticleEmitterOn();
    }

    touch_start( integer num )
    {
        // uncomment the following line to allow this effect to be
turned off
        //state off;
    }
}

state off
{
    state_entry()
    {
        generalParticleEmitterOff();
    }

    touch_start( integer num )
    {
        state default;
    }
}
```

The only changes made to the Basic Particle Emitter script were to the function. Several of the parameters to the function call were changed.

Table 12.4: Fog Machine Attributes

Particle Attribute	Value
PSYS_PART_FLAGS	PSYS_PART_INTERP_COLOR_MASK, PSYS_PART_INTERP_SCALE_MASK, PSYS_PART_FOLLOW_SRC_MASK, PSYS_PART_FOLLOW_VELOCITY_ MASK, and PSYS_PART_EMISSIVE_ MASK.
PSYS_SRC_PATTERN	PSYS_SRC_PATTERN_ANGLE_CONE
PSYS_SRC_TEXTURE	""
PSYS_SRC_MAX_AGE	0.0
PSYS_PART_MAX_AGE	10.0
PSYS_SRC_BURST_RATE	0.2
PSYS_SRC_BURST_PART_COUNT	2
PSYS_SRC_BURST_RADIUS	10.0
PSYS_SRC_BURST_SPEED_MIN	.1
PSYS_SRC_BURST_SPEED_MAX	.1
PSYS_SRC_ACCEL	<0,0,0.05>
PSYS_PART_START_COLOR	<1,1,1>
PSYS_PART_END_COLOR	<1,1,1>
PSYS_PART_START_ALPHA	0.1
PSYS_PART_END_ALPHA	0.1
PSYS_PART_START_SCALE	<15,15,15>
PSYS_PART_END_SCALE	<5,5,5>
PSYS_SRC_ANGLE_BEGIN	0 * DEG_TO_RAD
PSYS_SRC_ANGLE_END	360 * DEG_TO_RAD
PSYS_SRC_OMEGA	<0.0,0.0,0.0>

To create fog, a large particle is selected. The particles start at and end at . Additionally, they are emitted for the full 360 degrees of a 3D cone. The fog particles are allowed to remain for up to ten seconds. However, two new fog particles are emitted five times a second. The fog is emitted with very low speed and acceleration parameters. These parameters produce a lingering fog effect.

Snowflake Emitter

So far the particles have been solid color masses. It is also possible to use a texture for the particle. This allows you to create particles that resemble real-world objects. A snowflake is a real-world object that makes a useful particle. This section will show you how to modify the Basic Particle emitter script to produce snowflakes.

The snowflake texture is a simple transparent snowflake, as can be seen in Figure 12.3.

Figure 12.3: Snowflake Texture

These snowflakes will be much smaller than Figure 12.3 when emitted. Figure 12.4 shows a snowflake emitter working.

Figure 12.4: A Snowflake Emitter

The script used to create the snowflake emitter is an adaptation of the Basic Particle emitter script, shown in Listing 12.1. The snowflake emitter can be seen in Listing 12.3.

Listing 12.3: snowflake Emitter

```
generalParticleEmitterOn()
{
    llParticleSystem([
        PSYS_PART_FLAGS , 0
    //| PSYS_PART_BOUNCE_MASK         //Bounce on object's z-axis
    | PSYS_PART_WIND_MASK             //Particles are moved by wind
    | PSYS_PART_INTERP_COLOR_MASK     //Colors fade from start to
end
    | PSYS_PART_INTERP_SCALE_MASK     //Scale fades from beginning
to end
    | PSYS_PART_FOLLOW_SRC_MASK       //Particles follow the emitter
    | PSYS_PART_FOLLOW_VELOCITY_MASK  //Particles are created at the
velocity of the emitter
    //| PSYS_PART_TARGET_POS_MASK     //Particles follow the target
    | PSYS_PART_EMISSIVE_MASK         //Particles are self-lit
```

```
(glow)
    //| PSYS_PART_TARGET_LINEAR_MASK//Undocumented--Sends parti-
cles in straight line?
    ,

    //PSYS_SRC_TARGET_KEY , NULL_KEY,//The particles will head to-
wards the specified key
    //Select one of the following for a pattern:
    //PSYS_SRC_PATTERN_DROP               Particles start at
emitter with no velocity
    //PSYS_SRC_PATTERN_EXPLODE            Particles explode from
the emitter
    //PSYS_SRC_PATTERN_ANGLE              Particles are emitted
in a 2-D angle
    //PSYS_SRC_PATTERN_ANGLE_CONE         Particles are emitted
in a 3-D cone
    //PSYS_SRC_PATTERN_ANGLE_CONE_EMPTY   Particles are emitted
everywhere except for a 3-D cone

    PSYS_SRC_PATTERN,           PSYS_SRC_PATTERN_ANGLE_CONE

    ,PSYS_SRC_TEXTURE,          "snowflake"          //UUID of
the desired particle texture, or inventory name
    ,PSYS_SRC_MAX_AGE,          0.0           //Time, in sec-
onds, for particles to be emitted. 0 = forever
    ,PSYS_PART_MAX_AGE,         60.0          //Lifetime, in
seconds, that a particle lasts
    ,PSYS_SRC_BURST_RATE,       0.2           //How long, in
seconds, between each emission
    ,PSYS_SRC_BURST_PART_COUNT, 20            //Number of par-
ticles per emission
    ,PSYS_SRC_BURST_RADIUS,     10.0          //Radius of emis-
sion
    ,PSYS_SRC_BURST_SPEED_MIN,  1.0           //Minimum speed
of an emitted particle
    ,PSYS_SRC_BURST_SPEED_MAX,  2.0           //Maximum speed
of an emitted particle
    ,PSYS_SRC_ACCEL,            <0,0,-0.5>    //Acceleration of
particles each second
    ,PSYS_PART_START_COLOR,     <1,1,1> //Starting RGB color
    ,PSYS_PART_END_COLOR,       <1,1,1> //Ending RGB color, if
INTERP_COLOR_MASK is on
    ,PSYS_PART_START_ALPHA,     1.0           //Starting trans-
parency, 1 is opaque, 0 is transparent.
    ,PSYS_PART_END_ALPHA,       1.0           //Ending transpar-
ency
```

```
    ,PSYS_PART_START_SCALE,        <0.25,0.25,0.25>  //Starting par-
ticle size
    ,PSYS_PART_END_SCALE,          <0.25,0.25,0.25>  //Ending par-
ticle size, if INTERP_SCALE_MASK is on
    ,PSYS_SRC_ANGLE_BEGIN,         0 * DEG_TO_RAD //Inner angle for
ANGLE patterns
    ,PSYS_SRC_ANGLE_END,           360 * DEG_TO_RAD//Outer angle for
ANGLE patterns
    ,PSYS_SRC_OMEGA,               <0.0,0.0,0.0>  //Rotation of
ANGLE patterns, similar to llTargetOmega()
            ]);
}

generalParticleEmitterOff()
{
    llParticleSystem([]);
}

default
{
    state_entry()
    {
        generalParticleEmitterOn();
    }

    touch_start( integer num )
    {
        // uncomment the following line to allow this effect to be
turned off
        //state off;
    }
}

state off
{
    state_entry()
    {
        generalParticleEmitterOff();
    }

    touch_start( integer num )
    {
        state default;
    }
}
```

The only changes made to the Basic Particle Emitter script were to the function. Several of the parameters to the function call were changed. These changes are summarized in Table 12.5.

Table 12.5: Snowflake Emitter Attributes

Particle Attribute	Value
PSYS_PART_FLAGS	PSYS_PART_WIND_MASK, PSYS_PART_INTERP_COLOR_MASK, PSYS_PART_INTERP_SCALE_MASK, PSYS_PART_FOLLOW_SRC_MASK, PSYS_PART_FOLLOW_VELOCITY_MASK, PSYS_PART_EMISSIVE_MASK
PSYS_SRC_PATTERN	PSYS_SRC_PATTERN_ANGLE_CONE
PSYS_SRC_TEXTURE	"snowflake"
PSYS_SRC_MAX_AGE	0.0
PSYS_PART_MAX_AGE	60.0
PSYS_SRC_BURST_RATE	0.2
PSYS_SRC_BURST_PART_COUNT	20
PSYS_SRC_BURST_RADIUS	10.0
PSYS_SRC_BURST_SPEED_MIN	1.0
PSYS_SRC_BURST_SPEED_MAX	2.0
PSYS_SRC_ACCEL	<0,0,-0.5>
PSYS_PART_START_COLOR	<1,1,1>
PSYS_PART_END_COLOR	<1,1,1>
PSYS_PART_START_ALPHA	1.0
PSYS_PART_END_ALPHA	1.0
PSYS_PART_START_SCALE	<0.25,0.25,0.25>
PSYS_PART_END_SCALE	<0.25,0.25,0.25>
PSYS_SRC_ANGLE_BEGIN	0 * DEG_TO_RAD
PSYS_SRC_ANGLE_END	360 * DEG_TO_RAD
PSYS_SRC_OMEGA	<0.0,0.0,0.0>

To create snowflake, a small particle is selected. The particles start at and remains at that size. Additionally, they are emitted for the full 360 degrees of a 3D cone. The snowflakes particles are allowed to remain for up to a minute. However, twenty new snowflake particles are emitted five times a second. The snowflakes are emitted with very low speed and acceleration parameters. These parameters produce a gently falling snow effect.

Summary

Particles are 2D sprites that are displayed in the Second Life world. They can be used to create effects such as smoke, snow, fog, flashes and other effects. Particles are configured through a large set of parameters.

This is the final chapter of this book. There is likely to be future editions as Second Life evolves. We are always looking for suggestions and additional examples for future books. If you have any suggestions or comments on this book feel free to contact us at support@heatonresearch.com.

This book introduced you to the Linden Scripting Language. You now have the basic tools to begin building scripts of your own. If you are interested in learning more, you should consider purchasing our book "Scripting Recipes for Second Life" (ISBN 160439000X). This book contains scripting examples for many common objects in Second Life. The recipes span a wide array of uses. Useful recipes for buildings provide elevators, teleport pads and locking doors. Vehicles are covered with example cars, boats and helicopters. The video game side of Second Life is demonstrated with an assortment of gun and bullet recipes. Recipes for wearable items such as glittering jewelry, jet packs, parachutes and anti-push orbs are also presented. Recipes for slide shows, cannons, weather stations and other miscellaneous items are also covered. Commerce is a huge part of Second Life. Two chapters are dedicated to commerce objects, such as tip jars, rental scripts and vendor kiosks.

Heaton Research occasionally schedules classes in the Second Life world. These are almost always free of charge. To keep up to date on our Second Life events, consider joining the Second Life Group:

Heaton Research Courses

Simply search for it under groups! We hope you find these examples useful. Happy scripting!

Stop by and visit Heaton Research in Second Life. We own the island of Encogia, which can be found at the following URL:

http://slurl.com/secondlife/Encogia/197/191/23

Happy scripting!

APPENDIX A: DOWNLOADING EXAMPLES

This book contains many source code examples. You do not need to retype any of these examples; they all can be downloaded from the Internet.

Simply go to the site:

http://www.heatonresearch.com/download/

This site will give you more information on how to download the example programs.

All examples in this book can also be obtained as actual Second Life objects. This is done inside of Second Life itself. The examples can be found at the Heaton Research Tree House. Stop by and visit Heaton Research in Second Life. We own the island of Encogia, which can be found at the following URL:

http://slurl.com/secondlife/Encogia/197/191/23

INDEX

A

Acceleration 167
  of particles 203, 210, 215
Addition operator 131
Agent 55, 117, 172, 175, 183-4
Air 145-6, 186
ALPHA 203, 210, 212, 215, 217
Angle 41, 166, 177, 203-4, 206, 208, 210-1, 215-6
  patterns 204, 208, 211, 216
Angular 166, 171-4, 177, 179-82
  deflection 178-9, 181
  velocity 180
Applying Force 163, 166
Arrays 128, 131, 138, 218
  dimensional 138
Arrows 37-8, 76, 143
Attraction 172, 180, 182
Attributes 36-7, 186, 189, 191, 196-9
Automobile 51-2
Avatar
  radars 116
  touching 107, 126
Avatars 45, 51, 56-7, 60, 63-4, 99-108, 111, 113-21, 125-6, 155, 159-61, 163, 165-7, 174-5, 183-4
  bump 167
  communicate 99, 100
  detected 118
  female 159
  multiple 115
  touching 126, 128

B

Backwards 69, 174, 176, 181
Balloon 147-50, 152-7, 159, 161, 178
  seating script 159-60
  touring 147-9, 152
    hot-air 147
BANKING 179
Basic Particle 201-2, 205, 212-4, 217
Boing sound 164-5
Boolean 94, 191
  logic 65
Bounce 165, 178-80, 202, 205, 209, 214

Box 42, 46, 52, 110, 143, 192-5
Break 67-8
Building 35, 47, 51, 218
Bumper sticker 170
BUOYANCY Value 179
BURST 203, 207, 210, 212, 215, 217
Buttons 35, 52, 104, 109-11
  green 109
  red 109-10

C

Camera 178
Car 168, 176-8, 182
Card 118
Case statements 63, 66-8
Change 37, 40, 42, 120, 144, 146, 156, 170, 172, 174, 181, 183-4, 189, 192, 198
Channel 57, 64, 99-104, 111, 119-20
  chat 111
  normal conversation 101
  private 57
  special communications 99
CHANNEL variable 101
Characters 86-8, 96
  length of 87-8
CHARS 85, 87-8
Click 35-6
Code 51, 54, 56, 58, 66-7, 71, 77-8, 83, 95, 116, 124, 131-4, 146, 167-8, 170
  blocks of 54, 56, 63, 66-8, 71
  default block of 54
  following 55, 58-9, 64-6, 84, 197
Collides 113-5
Collision 51, 114-6, 163-5
  events 113-5
  script 115
  set 114
  stops 114-5
  track 114
Collision Start 115
Collisions work 115
Colon 95-6
Colors 42-3, 47, 55, 103, 108-11, 132, 134, 189, 191, 197-8

Comma-separated values 134
Commands 78, 100, 167
Commas 134-5, 149, 155
Communicate 52, 56-7, 99, 100, 102, 108, 111, 134
Communication 57, 97, 99, 101-3, 105, 107-9, 111, 134, 139
Communication Function Distance 102
Communication functions 102
Compare 67, 84, 86-90
  numerical integer values 67
CompareLen 86-7, 89, 90
  method 89, 90
CompareNoCase 86, 90
  function works 89
CompareNoCaseLen 86, 88-9
Comparison 64-5, 87, 89, 90
  direct string 52
Components 144-5, 198
Concept 52, 75
CONE 203, 206, 210, 212, 215, 217-8
Configuration information 92-7, 155
Configure Balloon 149, 153
Conjunction 44, 63, 65
Constants 101, 146, 163, 167, 189-92, 194, 196-7
Content 40, 44, 91, 118
  properties 43-4
  tab 44, 52
Control
  event handler 176-7
  keys 176
Conversations 100-1, 111
Coordinate planes 176
Coordinates 141, 143-6, 157, 159, 161, 185
  start 143
Core string operations 83
Count 57-60, 71, 137, 201, 203, 210, 212, 215, 217
  backwards 69
  maximum object 201
  variable 58
Countdown 152, 156
  state 156
Counters 58, 167
Creating Primitive Objects 35
Creating Vehicles 163
Creator 40
CSV 134-5
  functions 134, 136
  special form of 134
  string 134-5
Cube 52, 109, 111, 197
Curly brace 54
Current position 144-6, 157

CurrentWaypoint 149-50, 153-4, 157
Cursor keys 174, 176
Cylinder integer holeshape 193
Cylinders 193-5

D

Data, removing 131-2
Dataserver 93, 95, 150, 154
Decay 171, 179-81
  exponential 180
Decisions 61, 63, 70-1
Deflection 171, 178-9, 181
Degrees 41, 117, 146-7, 194, 196, 212, 218
Delimiter 135-6
Dialog 99, 103-4, 120-2
  lists 120
  payment 120-1
Direction 37, 146, 173-4, 176-7, 180, 185
Display 57-9, 71, 94, 108, 133-4, 145, 153
  function 59
Driver 170, 174, 182-3

E

Edit 39-41, 44, 52-3, 189
  window 194
Editing 36-40
Effectiveness 179-80
Efficiency 171-2, 181-2
Efficiency Value 179-80
Elements
  first 138, 197
  single 134
Emission 203, 207, 210, 215
Emitter 202-3, 205-6, 209-10, 214-5
  snowflake 213-4
EMPTY Particles 206
Encogia Island 142-4, 146, 148, 161, 218
END 203-4, 207-8, 210-2, 215-7
End-of-file 95, 154
Ending
  particle size 204, 208, 211, 216
  transparency 203, 207, 210, 215
Entry 57-60, 76-9, 90, 92-5, 105-6, 116-7, 123, 146-7, 149-50, 152, 154-7, 159-60, 164-5, 183-5, 204
EOF 93, 95, 150, 154-5
Event
  dataserver 95, 155

entry 58, 60, 64, 78-9, 101, 114, 177, 182
  functions 60, 113
  handler 101, 104, 165, 174
    changed 174, 184
  listen 64, 101, 113, 125
  message 111
  money 113, 119-20
  types 52, 60, 113
Events 52, 56, 58, 60, 78-9, 95, 107-8, 111, 113-7, 119, 121, 123-5, 127-9, 154, 163
  changed 160
  running 156
  single 156
Execute 44, 63, 65-6, 68, 70-1, 80, 133
EXPLODE Particles 206
Exponential timescale 179-80
Expression 55, 65, 68, 70-1

F

File 95, 97
  configuration 92
Fly 132, 144-5
Flying 148
Fog 212, 218
  machine 201, 208-9
Format 132, 134, 189
Friction 42, 169-72, 178, 180-2, 191, 196
Full-Bright 191
Func-function 139
Function call 102, 108, 138-9, 161, 167, 178, 184, 189
  single 132
Functionality 61, 77
Functions 52, 56-61, 80, 83-4, 87-8, 90, 101-2, 104, 107, 115-7, 120-1, 125, 128, 134-5, 205
  chapters 198
  compare 89
  compareLen 87, 89
  compareNoCase 89
  compareNoCaseLen 88
  complex 189
  generalParticleEmitterOn 212, 217
  global 153
  group detection 116
  nextWaypoint 154
  return 106
  simple 58, 120, 124
  single 57
  specialized 198
  updateText 120

G

GeneralParticleEmitterOff 204, 211, 216
GeneralParticleEmitterOn 202, 204-5, 209, 211, 214, 216
Getting List Statistics 137
Giver 119-20
Glass 42, 169-70
Glow 199, 202, 205, 210, 214
Gravity 42, 51, 115, 167, 191
Greeting 101
Ground 52, 114, 143, 145, 167, 169-70, 178
Group 125-8, 138, 218
  strided 138
Guessing game 122

H

Handler 174, 176
Heterogeneous list 55
Hole 194-5
Holesize 194
Hollow 41, 194
Hover 178-9
Hubcaps 185

I

Id 93, 95, 120, 124, 150, 154, 156
Impulse 163, 166-7
  vector 166
IMs 99
Index 85, 87-8, 92, 94, 133, 139, 153
Instant messages 99, 100, 102, 104-5, 111
Instructing avatars 106
Integer 55-60, 69-71, 76-9, 86, 89, 92-5, 104-6, 109-10, 115-7, 119, 122-5, 127, 133-5, 164-8, 191-2
Intensity 42, 189, 191
Interact 48, 61, 139, 141
Interval 113-4, 118, 123, 156
Inventory 91, 106, 118, 146
Island 148
Items 52, 92-6, 118, 128, 131-2, 134, 138-9, 165, 199
  inventory 55
  miscellaneous 218
  named 94
  pairs of 153, 155

removing 131
single 139
wearable 218

K

Key 55, 63-4, 101-6, 109-10, 116-9, 123, 126, 133, 153, 155, 159-61, 164-5, 203, 210, 215

L

Ladder 66-7
Land 35, 114-5, 142, 186, 201
  collision events 114
    parallel 114
  collisions 114-5
Language 52, 75, 128
Linden Scripting Language 48, 50-2, 60-4, 66-8, 70-2, 74-8, 80, 82-4, 96, 98-104, 128, 134-6, 138-40, 160-2, 188-90
Linden String Functions 84
Line 71, 93, 95-6, 124, 132-4, 149-50, 153-5, 168
Link 46, 110-1, 152, 155, 170
Linked
  messages 99, 108, 111
  prims 44, 108, 111, 196-7
Linking Primitive Objects 35
List 55, 66, 83-4, 87, 104, 117-8, 128, 131-9, 141, 155, 189-90, 194-8, 205
  temp 150, 155
  temporary 132
  test 139
  tracks 118
  waypoint 156
  waypoints 149, 153
List Statistics 136
Listen 64, 97, 100-2, 104, 108, 111, 120, 123
llApplyImpulse 167-8
llApplyRotationalImpulse 168
llAvatarOnSitTarget 159-60, 172, 175, 183-4
llCSV2List 135, 150, 155
llDeleteSubList 118, 132
llDeleteSubString 84
llDetectedKey 104-6, 116-8, 120, 124-6, 164-5
llDetectedName 105-7, 115-6, 125, 127-8
llDialog 104, 120
llDumpList2String 84, 132-3, 135
  using 135
llEuler2Rot 145, 147
llFabs 150-1, 157-8

llFrand 122, 125, 198
llGetListLength 118, 134, 149, 153
llGetMass 167-8
llGetNotecardLine 93, 95-6, 149-50, 154-5
llGetOwner 102, 119-20, 123-5, 133, 172, 175
llGetPos 135, 144-6, 150, 157, 198
  object call 144
llGetRegionName 105-6
llGetRot 145, 147
  object call 144
llGetSubString 85, 87, 93, 96
  extracts 84
llGetVel 168, 173, 176, 184-5
llGiveInventory 118
llGiveMoney 124
llInsertString 84
llInstantMessage 102, 105-7
llKey2Name 102, 119-20
llList2String 133
llList2CSV 135
llList2Integer Retrieve 133
llList2String 133-4, 149-50, 153, 155, 197
llList2String Retrieve 133
llList2Vector 133, 149, 153
llListen 63-4, 101, 103, 119, 123
  function call 64
llListFindList 117-8, 139
llListRandomize 138-9
llListSort 138-9
llListStatistics 137
llOwnerSay 102, 104, 133-5, 146
llParseString2List 84
llParseString2List Parse 136
llParseStringKeepNulls 84
llParseStringKeepNulls Parse 136
llParticleSystem 202, 204-5, 208-9, 211, 214, 216
  function call 208, 212, 217
llPreloadSound 164-5, 171, 178
llPushObject 164-6, 172, 175
llRegionSay 102
llRequestPermissions 123-4, 172, 175
llResetScript 105-6, 119, 123, 173, 176
llRot2Euler 145, 147
llSay 45, 56-60, 64-71, 76-9, 86, 90, 92-5, 101-2, 114-6, 119-20, 123, 125, 137, 145, 149-56
  function 102
    call 56
llSensorRepeat 117
llSetColor 104, 110-1
llSetForce 167
llSetLinkPrimitiveParams 189, 197
  function set 199

llSetPayPrice   121
llSetPos   146, 151, 159, 198
  function   157
llSetPrimitiveParams   189-91, 196-8
llSetRot   146-7
llSetScale   159-61
llSetSitText   159-60, 171, 177
llSetStatus   167, 170, 172, 175
llSetText   105-6, 108, 117, 119-20, 159-61
  function call   107
llSetTextureAnim   184-6
llSetTimerEvent   113-4, 123, 146-7, 150, 152, 156-
      7, 184-5, 198
  call   114
llSetVehicleFloatParam   171-2, 178, 181-2
llSetVehicleRotationParam   178
llSetVehicleType   171, 178, 181
llSetVehicleVectorParam   171, 173-4, 176-8, 181-2
llSitTarget   159-60, 171, 177, 183-4
  function call   182
llSleep   172, 175
llStringLength   84, 86, 89
llStringTrim   84
llSubStringIndex   85, 87, 93, 95
  fi nds   84
llTakeControls   173-4
llTargetOmega   147, 173, 175-6, 204, 211, 216
llToLower   84-6, 89, 90, 101, 104
llTriggerSound   116, 164-5, 172, 175
llUnSit   172, 175, 183-4
llVecMag   173, 176, 184-5
llWhisper   102, 105-6
Local variables   56-7, 157
Location   95-6, 132, 141, 146, 154, 166
Loop   63, 68-71, 87-8, 107, 115, 126, 133, 184-6
  executes   71
  types   68, 71
  works   71
Looping   88, 118, 137
Loops   63, 68, 70-1

M

Magic wand   36
Main Car Script   171
Mainland   142
Males   159
Map   141-2
  bump   195
MASK   202-4, 209-12, 214-7
Mass   167, 169, 180, 196

Match   64, 68, 150-1, 157-9, 195
MATERIAL   191, 196
Material types   42, 169-70, 196
Materials   43, 147, 169-70, 196
MAX   137, 203, 207-8, 210, 212, 215, 217
Maximum strength   179
MaxList   118
MEDIAN   137
Message   64, 100-2, 104-6, 108-11, 113, 120, 123,
      146, 149, 151-3, 155-6, 159, 161, 171-2, 175
  string   171
Meters   117, 148, 167, 207
Modifying Primitive Objects   35
Money   113, 119, 121-2, 124
Motion   47, 51, 167, 176, 184
Motor   170, 173-4, 176-8
MOTOR   171, 173-4, 176-7, 179-81
  angular   176-7, 179, 181
  linear   176, 180-1
Mouse   36
Movement   42, 46, 108, 139, 157, 161, 167

N

New script button   44
Non-Physical Movement   139, 141, 143, 145, 147,
      149, 151, 153, 155, 157, 159, 161
Notecards   83, 91-7, 116-8, 148, 150, 152-4
  configuration   152-4
  folder   91
  loading   149, 153
  new   91

O

Object   40-4, 46-8, 52, 55-8, 90-1, 99-102, 104-10,
      113-20, 125-8, 137, 144-7, 163, 165-8, 186,
      191-2
  bigger   35
  building   35
  collision events   114
  commerce   218
  common   218
  complex   46
    Second Life   47
  compound   46
  created   141
  current   166-7
  inventory   118
  linked   46, 108-9, 161

mathematically perfect 41
move 141, 161, 186
moving 117
multiple 46, 114
non-moving 117
non-physical 147, 166
phantom 116
primitive 35
properties 41, 118, 186
  tab 41
  window 126
real-world 213
resemble real-world 213
resize 186
scripted 60
in Second Life 35, 44, 47, 100, 115, 186
security 116
single 52, 108
tab 41
text 160
type 91
  special 128
window 169
Object Prim Properties 41
Objects
  follow 141
  move 141
  owner 102
  shine 199
Offset 43, 178, 180, 194
OMEGA 204, 211-2, 216-7
One-dimensional 138
Online Detector 105-6
Opaque 203, 207, 210, 215
Operator 55, 60, 65, 117, 132, 205
Owner 35, 40-1, 91, 100, 102, 104-6, 120-1, 125-6, 133, 171-2, 175
  message 171

P

Pager 105-6
Paging 105-6
Pairs 139, 153-4
  name-value 205-6
Parameters 57-60, 64, 87-8, 101, 107-8, 110, 117, 121, 139, 147, 167, 189, 194, 212, 217-8
Parse 80, 83, 92, 94, 135, 155
Particle
  emission 201, 203, 207-8, 210, 215
  emitter script 208-9

basic 201, 208
emitters 201, 205, 207-8
script, basic 208
system 205, 208
Particles 199, 201-3, 205, 207-10, 213-5, 218
  fog 212
  follow 202, 209, 214
  large 212
  producing 208
  red 201, 208
  snowflake 218
  start 203, 206, 208, 210, 212, 215, 218
Parts, common 128
Passengers 147, 156, 159, 182-3
Pattern 203, 205, 210, 215
PATTERN 203, 206, 210, 212, 215, 217
Perm 123-4, 173-4
Permission event 124
Permissions 41, 121, 123-4, 172-5
  event handler 174
Physical
  movement 141, 144, 161, 163, 165, 167, 169, 171, 173, 175, 177, 179, 181, 183, 185
  objects 42, 46, 115, 166, 170, 175
Physics 141, 161, 163, 167, 169, 172, 175, 191
PI 117, 147, 173, 175, 192
Pos 145-6, 150-1, 157-9, 202, 205, 207, 209, 214
Primitive Object Properties 35
Primitive types 192, 194
Primitives 40, 51-2, 108, 170, 189, 192, 197-9
Primitive's Attributes 189
Primitives, geometric 36
Private islands 142
Prize 123, 125
Products 138-9
  list of 138-9
Program 35, 48, 52, 72, 75, 80, 87, 108, 125
  computer 48, 75
Programming 75, 77-8
  languages 52, 68, 128, 131
Properties 39-41

Q

Quaternions 145, 161

R

Radians 117, 146-7, 161, 208
RADIUS 203, 210, 212, 215, 217

Random values   198
Randomize   138-9
Randomizing Lists   138
Range   136-7, 189, 194, 201
RATE   203, 210, 212, 215, 217
Ratio   171, 173-4, 177
Read   91-2, 94-7, 153-4
  notecards   92
Recipes   102, 218
Regions   102, 141-5, 147, 157, 161
  large grid of   141-2
Reset   57-8, 106, 120, 154, 157
Resize boxes   37-8
RGB color   203, 207, 210, 215
Root prim   46-7, 108, 110, 170-1, 183, 197
Rotation
  current   144-5, 147, 168
  objects   145
  rot   145, 147, 191
  values   197
Rotational   168
Rubber   42, 169, 191

S

Sandbox   35
Scan   117
Scanners   117
Scope   56-7, 145
Script   43-5, 51-8, 60-1, 63-4, 70-1, 75-80, 90-2, 94, 101-11, 113-5, 117-9, 124-6, 145-7, 185-6, 197-9
  active   189
  building   218
  complex   45
  editor   53-4
  executes   80
  following   56-7, 59, 70, 77-8, 101, 125-7
  functionality   165
  generic   54
  hubcap   185
  level variables   56-8, 94, 105
  new   44-5, 52-4, 76
  notecard   94
  programming   61
  rental   218
  segment   68, 80
    following   65, 67-8, 79
  sets   71
  variables   79, 96
  vehicle   170

  wheel   185
Seconds   152, 156, 181, 197-8, 203, 207, 210, 212, 215
Self-lit   202, 205, 209, 214
Send   99, 100, 102, 104-6, 109-10
  instant messages   97, 100, 104, 111
  seat scripts   155
Sends particles   203, 210, 215
Sensor Events   113, 116, 118
Sensors   116-7
Set   35, 40-2, 44, 77, 95-6, 126, 147, 156-8, 167, 177-8, 180-1, 189, 191, 196-8, 208
  empty   208
  link   197, 199
Setting   127, 160, 169, 176-7, 181, 198
Shininess   43, 191, 196
Shorthand   55
Signature   108, 114, 117, 119, 121, 124, 136, 138-9, 166, 168, 189, 197
Simple Notecard   92
Simulate   51
Simulation   51
Size, particle   203, 208, 211
Smoke   199, 201, 218
Snowflakes   213, 215, 218
Snowman   46-7
Sorting   138
Sorting Lists   138
Sounds   51-2, 55, 165, 175, 178
Speak   100, 111
Sphere   192-4
  integer holeshape   193
Spins   147, 166, 168
Sprites   199, 201, 218
Squares   136-7, 195
Src   133
Start   45, 54, 56-60, 69-71, 76-9, 104-6, 109-10, 114-6, 133-5, 145, 164-5, 171-2, 202-5, 207-12, 214-7
  event function   58, 104, 126
Starting
  point   54, 201
  transparency   203, 207, 210, 215
STAT   136-7
State
  engines   75, 80
  level variables   79
  loading   92-5
  machines   52, 54, 72, 75-81
    in Second Life   75
  multiple   60
  mystate   79, 80

statement 78
switches 78
Statements 60, 63-8, 71
  break 67
  control 63, 71
  default 68
  return 60
  special 66
  switch 67-8
Statistic Type Purpose 136
Statistic Types 136
Statistics 136-7
Stop 167-8, 170, 175, 181, 208, 218
Strided lists 131, 133, 138-9, 141
String 55-60, 69-71, 80, 83-91, 94, 96-7, 101-2,
    105, 110, 119-20, 123, 131-7, 139, 145-6,
    149
Sum 136, 180
Switch 63, 66-8, 71, 77-8
Symbols 134

T

Tabs 40-1
Taper 41, 194
Target vector 153, 159
Temp 150, 155, 191
Terminal state 76
Text 83, 91, 96, 106-8, 120, 160, 177
Texture 40, 43-4, 55, 185, 189, 192, 195, 203, 208,
    210, 212-3, 215, 217
  desired particle 203, 207, 210, 215
  snowflake 213
Thanks for the 119-20
Timer 113-4, 124, 146-7, 150, 152, 156-7, 184-5,
    198
  event 113, 147, 156-7, 198
Timer Events 52, 113
Timescale 171-2, 179-82
Timescale Exponential timescale 179
Timescales 180
Tip jars 119-20, 218
Tips 120
Tires 169, 185
Tom 139
Tools menu 46
Top 80, 109-10, 144
TORUS 193
Torus integer holeshape 193
Touch 45, 56-60, 69-71, 76-9, 102, 104-7, 109-10,
    113, 119, 124-7, 133-5, 145, 204, 211, 216

events 103, 109
  named 54
Touching 126
  avatar claims 106
Tours 147, 149, 161
Trampoline 163-5
Trampoline Script 164
Tube integer hole-shape 194
Tubes 194
Turn 51, 169, 174-6, 178, 181
Twist 41, 194
Types
  common loop 68
  numeric 56
  third loop 71
  vector data 108, 161

U

UpdateText 119-20
Url 84, 218
User 52, 77, 99, 101, 103-6, 119-21, 124, 127, 155,
    159, 176-7, 183
UUID 55, 203, 207, 210, 215

V

Values 55-60, 64, 69-71, 77, 87-8, 92-4, 96, 108,
    138, 146-7, 149, 153, 180-1, 189, 206-8
Vector 55, 108, 131, 133-4, 144-7, 149-50, 155,
    161, 164-5, 167-8, 172, 175, 191-4, 197-8,
    208
  acceleration 207
  vel 173, 176, 184-5
  vrot 145, 147
  zero 133
VEHICLE 171-4, 176-82
  axes 180
  creation 170
  parameters 178, 181
  shares 177
Vehicle Materials 169
Vehicle Motors 163, 167
Vehicle Type Purpose 178
Vehicle Types 177-8, 181
Vehicle z-axis 180
Vehicles 42, 46, 51, 125, 163, 165, 167, 169-71,
    173-87, 201, 218
  advanced 161
  in Second Life 176

Vel   173, 176, 184-5
Velocity   167-8, 179, 202-3, 205-6, 209-10, 214-5
VELOCITY   202, 205, 209, 212, 214, 217
Velocity, linear   180-1
Vrot   145, 147

W

Waiting state   152, 155-6, 159
Water   116, 178
Waypoint message   159
Waypoints   149-50, 152-5, 157, 159
  balloon loading   149, 154
  list   153, 155
  next   153, 157, 159
Weather stations   218
Welcome Notecard   117
West   142, 144
Wheels   172, 184-5
WheelScript.lsl   184-5
Wind   42, 191, 202, 205, 209, 214
WIND   202, 205, 209, 214, 217
Window   35-6, 46
Wood   42, 169, 196
World   48, 51, 61, 64, 97, 106, 139, 141
  z-axis   180

X

X-coordinate   146, 157
X-Rotation   145

Y

Y-coordinate   158, 181
Y-Rotation   145

Z

Z-axis   147, 180, 202, 205, 209, 214
Z-coordinates   108, 143-4, 146, 149, 158, 161, 166-
      8, 177, 181
Z-Rotation   145